W9-ANM-413

A Tour on the Prairies

A Tour on the Prairies

Thirty Days in Deep Indian Country

Washington Irving

Skyhorse Publishing

Copyright © 2013 by Skyhorse Publishing

All Rights Reserved. No part of this book may be reproduced in any manner without the express written consent of the publisher, except in the case of brief excerpts in critical reviews or articles. All inquiries should be addressed to Skyhorse Publishing, 307 West 36th Street, 11th Floor, New York, NY 10018.

Skyhorse Publishing books may be purchased in bulk at special discounts for sales promotion, corporate gifts, fund-raising, or educational purposes. Special editions can also be created to specifications. For details, contact the Special Sales Department, Skyhorse Publishing, 307 West 36th Street, 11th Floor, New York, NY 10018 or info@skyhorsepublishing.com.

Skyhorse® and Skyhorse Publishing® are registered trademarks of Skyhorse Publishing, Inc.®, a Delaware corporation.

Visit our website at www.skyhorsepublishing.com.

10 9 8 7 6 5 4 3 2 1

Library of Congress Cataloging-in-Publication Data is available on file.
ISBN: 978-1-62087-628-2

Printed in the United States of America

Contents

A TOUR ON THE PRAIRIES

INTRODUCTION

HAVING, since my return to the United States, made a wide and varied tour, for the gratification of my curiosity, it has been supposed that I did it for the purpose of writing a book; and it has more than once been intimated in the papers that such a work was actually in the press containing scenes and sketches of the Far West.

These announcements, gratuitously made for me, before I had put pen to paper, or even contemplated anything of the kind, have embarrassed me exceedingly. I have been like a poor actor, who finds himself announced for a part he had no thought of playing, and his appearance expected on the stage before he has committed a line to memory.

I have always had a repugnance, amounting almost to disability, to write in the face of expectation; and, in the present instance, I was expected to write about a region fruitful of wonders and adventures, and which had already been made the theme of spirit-stirring narratives from able pens; yet about which I had nothing wonderful or adventurous to offer.

Since such, however, seems to be the desire of the public, and that they take sufficient interest in my wanderings to deem them worthy of recital, I have hastened, as promptly as possible, to meet, in some degree, the expectation which others have excited. For this purpose I have, as it were, plucked a few leaves out of my memorandum book, containing a month's foray beyond the outposts of human habitation, into the wilderness of the Far West. It forms, indeed, but a small portion of an extensive tour; but it is an episode complete as far as it goes. As such, I offer it to the public, with great diffidence. It is a simple narrative of every day occurrences; such as happen to every one who travels the prairies. I have no wonders to describe, nor any moving accidents by flood or field to narrate; and as to those who look for a marvelous or adventurous story at my hands, I can only reply, in the words of the weary knife-grinder: "Story! God bless you, I have none to tell, sir."

CHAPTER ONE

THE PAWNEE HUNTING GROUNDS—TRAVELING COMPANIONS —A COMMISSIONER—A VIRTUOSO—A SEEKER OF ADVENTURES—A GIL BLAS OF THE FRONTIER—A YOUNG MAN'S ANTICIPATIONS OF PLEASURE

IN the often vaunted regions of the Far West, several hundred miles beyond the Mississippi, extends a vast tract of uninhabited country, where there is neither to be seen the log house of the white man nor the wigwam of the Indian. It consists of great grassy plains, interspersed with forests and groves, and clumps of trees, and watered by the Arkansas, the grand Canadian, the Red River, and their tributary streams. Over these fertile and verdant wastes still roam the elk, the buffalo, and the wild horse, in all their native freedom. These, in fact, are the hunting grounds of the various tribes of the Far West. Hither repair the Osage, the Creek, the Delaware and other tribes that have linked themselves with civilization, and live within the vicinity of the white settlements. Here resort, also, the Pawnees, the Comanches, and other fierce, and as yet independent tribes, the nomads of the prairies, or the inhabitants of the skirts of the Rocky Mountains. The regions I have mentioned form a debatable ground of these warring and vindictive tribes;

none of them presume to erect a permanent habitation within its borders. Their hunters and "Braves" repair thither in numerous bodies during the season of game, throw up their transient hunting camps, consisting of light bowers covered with bark and skins, commit sad havoc among the innumerable herds that graze the prairies, and having loaded themselves with venison and buffalo meat, warily retire from the dangerous neighborhood. These expeditions partake, always, of a warlike character; the hunters are all armed for action, offensive and defensive, and are bound to incessant vigilance. Should they, in their excursions, meet the hunters of an adverse tribe, savage conflicts take place. Their encampments, too, are always subject to be surprised by wandering war parties, and their hunters, when scattered in pursuit of game, to be captured or massacred by lurking foes. Mouldering skulls and skeletons, bleaching in some dark ravine, or near the traces of a hunting camp, occasionally mark the scene of a foregone act of blood, and let the wanderer know the dangerous nature of the region he is traversing. It is the purport of the following pages to narrate a month's excursion to these noted hunting grounds, through a tract of country which had not as yet been explored by white men.

It was early in October, 1832, that I arrived at Fort Gibson, a frontier post of the Far West, situated on the Neosho, or Grand River, near its confluence with the Arkansas. I had been traveling for a month past, with a small party from St. Louis, up the banks of the Missouri, and along the frontier line of agencies and missions that extends from the Missouri to the Arkansas. Our party was headed by one of the Commissioners appointed by the government of the United States to superintend the settlement of the Indian tribes migrating from the east to the west of the Mississippi. In the discharge of his duties, he was thus visiting the various outposts of civilization.

And here let me bear testimony to the merits of this worthy leader of our little band. He was a native of one of the towns of Connecticut, a man in whom a course of legal practice and political life had not been able to vitiate an innate simplicity and benevolence of heart. The greater part of his days had been passed in the bosom of his family and the society of deacons, elders, and selectmen, on the peaceful banks of the Connecticut; when suddenly he had been called to mount his steed, shoulder his rifle, and mingle among stark hunters, backwoodsmen, and naked savages, on the trackless wilds of the Far West.

Another of my fellow-travelers was Mr. L., an Englishman by birth, but descended from a foreign stock; and who had all the buoyancy and accommodating spirit of a native of the Continent. Having rambled over many countries, he had become, to a certain degree, a citizen of the world, easily adapting himself to any change. He was a man of a thousand occupations; a botanist, a geologist, a hunter of beetles and butterflies, a musical amateur, a sketcher of no mean pretensions, in short, a complete virtuoso; added to which, he was a very indefatigable, if not always a very successful, sportsman. Never had a man more irons in the fire, and, consequently, never was man more busy nor more cheerful.

My third fellow-traveler was one who had accompanied the former from Europe, and traveled with him as his Telemachus; being apt, like his prototype, to give occasional perplexity and disquiet to his Mentor. He was a young Swiss count, scarce twenty-one years of age, full of talent and spirit, but galliard in the extreme, and prone to every kind of wild adventure.

Having made this mention of my comrades, I must not pass over unnoticed a personage of inferior rank, but of all-pervading and prevalent importance: the squire, the groom, the cook, the tent man, in a word, the factotum, and, I may add, the universal meddler and marplot of our party. This was a little swarthy, meager, French creole named Antoine, but familiarly dubbed Tonish: a kind of Gil Blas of the frontier, who had passed a scrambling life, sometimes among white men, sometimes among Indians; sometimes in the employ of traders, missionaries, and Indian agents; sometimes mingling with the Osage hunters. We picked him up at St. Louis, near which he had a small farm, an Indian wife, and a brood of half-blood children. According to his own account, however, he had a wife in every tribe; in fact, if all this little vagabond said of himself were to be believed, he was without morals, without caste, without creed, without country, and even without language; for he spoke a jargon of mingled French, English, and Osage. He was, withal, a notorious braggart, and a liar of the first water. It was amusing to hear him vapor and gasconade about his terrible exploits and hairbreadth escapes in war and hunting. In the midst of his volubility, he was prone to be seized by a spasmodic gasping, as if the springs of his jaws were suddenly unhinged; but I am apt to think it was caused by some falsehood that stuck in his throat, for I generally remarked that immediately afterward there bolted forth a lie of the first magnitude.

Our route had been a pleasant one, quartering ourselves, occasionally, at the widely separated establishments of the Indian missionaries, but in general camping out in the fine groves that border the streams, and sleeping under cover of a tent. During the latter part of our tour we had pressed forward, in hopes of arriving in time at Fort Gibson to accompany the Osage hunters on their autumnal visit to the buffalo prairies. Indeed the imagination of the young count had become completely excited on the subject. The grand scenery and wild habits of the prairies had set his spirits madding, and the stories that little Tonish told him of Indian braves and Indian beauties, of hunting buffaloes and catching wild horses, had set him all agog for a dash into savage life. He was a bold and hard rider, and longed to be scouring the hunting grounds. It was amusing to hear his youthful anticipations of all that he was to see, and do, and enjoy, when mingling among the Indians and participating in their hardy adventures; and it was still more amusing to listen to the gasconadings of little Tonish, who volunteered to be his faithful squire in all his perilous undertakings; to teach him how to catch the wild horse, bring down the buffalo, and win the smiles of Indian princesses—"And if we can only get sight of a prairie on fire!" said the young count—"By Gar, I'll set one on fire myself!" cried the little Frenchman.

CHAPTER TWO

ANTICIPATIONS DISAPPOINTED—NEW PLANS—PREPARATIONS TO JOIN AN EXPLORING PARTY—DEPARTURE FROM FORT GIBSON—FORDING OF THE VERDIGRIS—AN INDIAN CAVALIER

THE anticipations of a young man are prone to meet with disappointment. Unfortunately for the count's scheme of wild campaigning, before we reached the end of our journey, we heard that the Osage hunters had set forth upon their expedition to the buffalo grounds. The count still determined, if possible, to follow on their track and overtake them, and for this purpose stopped short at the Osage Agency, a few miles distant from Fort Gibson, to make inquiries and preparations. His traveling companion, Mr. L., stopped with him; while the commissioner and myself proceeded to Fort Gibson, followed by the faithful and veracious Tonish. I hinted to him his promises to follow the count in his campaignings, but I found the little varlet had a keen eye to self-interest. He was aware that the commissioner, from his official duties, would remain for a long time in the country, and be likely to give him permanent employment, while the sojourn of the count would be but transient. The gasconading of the little braggart was suddenly therefore at an end. He spake not another word to the young count about Indians, buffaloes, and wild horses, but putting himself tacitly in the train of the commissioner, jogged silently after us to the garrison.

On arriving at the fort, however, a new chance presented

itself for a cruise on the prairies. We learned that a company of mounted rangers, or riflemen, had departed but three days previous to make a wide exploring tour from the Arkansas to the Red River, including a part of the Pawnee hunting grounds where no party of white men had as yet penetrated. Here, then, was an opportunity of ranging over those dangerous and interesting regions under the safeguard of a powerful escort; for the commissioner, in virtue of his office, could claim the service of this newly raised corps of riflemen, and the country they were to explore was destined for the settlement of some of the migrating tribes connected with his mission.

Our plan was promptly formed and put into execution. A couple of Creek Indians were sent off express, by the commander of Fort Gibson, to overtake the rangers and bring them to a halt until the commissioner and his party should be able to join them. As we should have a march of three or four days through a wild country before we could overtake the company of rangers, an escort of fourteen mounted riflemen, under the command of a lieutenant, was assigned us.

We sent word to the young count and Mr. L. at the Osage Agency of our new plan and prospects, and invited them to accompany us. The count, however, could not forego the delights he had promised himself in mingling with absolutely savage life. In reply, he agreed to keep with us until we should come upon the trail of the Osage hunters, when it was his fixed resolve to strike off into the wilderness in pursuit of them; and his faithful Mentor, though he grieved at the madness of the scheme, was too stanch a friend to desert him. A general rendezvous of our party and escort was appointed, for the following morning, at the Agency.

We now made all arrangements for prompt departure. Our baggage had hitherto been transported on a light wagon, but we were now to break our way through an untraveled country, cut up by rivers, ravines, and thickets, where a vehicle of the kind would be a complete impediment. We were to travel on horseback, in hunter's style, and with as little encumbrance as possible. Our baggage, therefore, underwent a rigid and most abstemious reduction. A pair of saddle-bags, and those by no means crammed, sufficed for each man's scanty wardrobe, and, with his greatcoat, were to be carried upon the steed he rode. The rest of the baggage was placed on pack-horses. Each one had a bear-skin and a couple of blankets for bedding, and there was a tent to shelter us in case of sickness or bad weather. We took care to provide ourselves with flour, coffee, and sugar, together with a small supply of salt pork for emergencies; for our main subsistence we were to depend upon the chase.

Such of our horses as had not been tired out in our recent journey were taken with us as pack-horses, or supernumeraries; but as we were going on a long and rough tour, where there would be occasional hunting, and where, in case of meeting with hostile savages, the safety of the rider might depend upon the goodness of his steed, we took care to be well mounted. I procured a stout silver-gray; somewhat rough, but stanch and powerful; and retained a hardy pony which I had hitherto ridden, and which, being somewhat jaded, was suffered to ramble along with the pack-horses, to be mounted only in case of emergency.

All these arrangements being made, we left Fort Gibson, on the morning of the tenth of October, and crossing the river in the front of it, set off for the rendezvous at the Agency. A ride of a few miles brought us to the ford of the Verdigris, a wild rocky scene overhung with forest trees. We descended to the bank of the river and crossed in straggling file, the horses stepping cautiously from rock to rock, and in a manner feeling about for a foothold beneath the rushing and brawling stream.

Our little Frenchman, Tonish, brought up the rear with the pack-horses. He was in high glee, having experienced a kind of promotion. In our journey hitherto he had driven the wagon, which he seemed to consider a very inferior employ; now he was master of the horse.

He sat perched like a monkey behind the pack on one of

the horses; he sang, he shouted, he yelped like an Indian, and ever and anon blasphemed the loitering pack-horses in his jargon of mingled French, English and Osage, which not one of them could understand.

As we were crossing the ford we saw on the opposite shore a Creek Indian on horseback. He had paused to reconnoiter us from the brow of a rock, and formed a picturesque object, in unison with the wild scenery around him. He wore a bright blue hunting-shirt trimmed with scarlet fringe; a gayly colored handkerchief was bound round his head something like a turban, with one end hanging down beside his ear; he held a long rifle in his hand, and looked like a wild Arab on the prowl. Our loquacious and ever-meddling little Frenchman called out to him in his Babylonish jargon, but the savage, having satisfied his curiosity, tossed his hand in the air, turned the head of his steed, and galloping along the shore soon disappeared among the trees.

CHAPTER THREE

AN INDIAN AGENCY—RIFLEMEN—OSAGES, CREEKS, TRAP-
PERS, DOGS, HORSES, HALF-BREEDS—BEATTE,
THE HUNTSMAN

HAVING crossed the ford, we soon reached the Osage Agency, where Colonel Choteau has his offices and magazines, for the dispatch of Indian affairs, and the distribution of presents and supplies. It consisted of a few log houses on the banks of the river, and presented a motley frontier scene. Here was our escort awaiting our arrival; some were on horseback, some on foot, some seated on the trunks of fallen trees, some shooting at a mark. They were a heterogeneous crew; some in frock-coats made of green blankets; others in leathern hunting-shirts, but the most part in marvelously ill-cut garments, much the worse for wear, and evidently put on for rugged service.

Near by these was a group of Osages: stately fellows; stern and simple in garb and aspect. They wore no ornaments; their dress consisted merely of blankets, leggings, and moccasins. Their heads were bare; their hair was cropped close, excepting a bristling ridge on the top, like the crest of a helmet, with a long scalp lock hanging behind. They had fine Roman countenances, and broad deep chests; and, as they generally wore their blankets wrapped round their loins, so as to leave the bust and arms bare, they looked like so many noble bronze figures. The Osages are the finest looking Indians I have ever seen in the West. They have not yielded sufficiently, as yet, to the influence of civilization to lay by their simple Indian garb, or to lose the habits of the hunter and the warrior; and their poverty prevents their indulging in much luxury of apparel.

In contrast to these was a gayly dressed party of Creeks. There is something, at the first glance, quite Oriental in the appearance of this tribe. They dress in calico hunting shirts, of various brilliant colors, decorated with bright fringes, and belted with broad girdles, embroidered with beads: they have leggings of dressed deer skins, or of green or scarlet cloth, with embroidered knee-bands and tassels: their moccasins are fancifully wrought and ornamented, and they wear gaudy handkerchiefs tastefully bound round their heads. .

Besides these, there was a sprinkling of trappers, hunters, half-breeds, creoles, negroes of every hue; and all that other rabble rout of nondescript beings that keep about the frontiers, between civilized and savage life, as those equivocal birds, the bats, hover about the confines of light and darkness.

The little hamlet of the Agency was in a complete bustle; the blacksmith's shed, in particular, was a scene of preparation; a strapping negro was shoeing a horse; two half-breeds were fabricating iron spoons in which to melt lead for bullets. An old trapper, in leathern hunting frock and moccasins, had placed his rifle against a work-bench, while he superintended the operation, and gossiped about his hunting exploits; several large dogs were lounging in and out of the shop, or sleeping in the sunshine, while a little cur, with head cocked on one side, and one ear erect, was watching, with that curiosity common to little dogs, the process of shoeing the horse, as if studying the art, or waiting for his turn to be shod.

We found the count and his companion, the virtuoso, ready for the march. As they intended to overtake the Osages, and pass some time in hunting the buffalo and the wild horse, they had provided themselves accordingly; having, in addition to the steeds which they used for traveling, others of prime quality, which were to be led when on the march, and only to be mounted for the chase.

They had, moreover, engaged the services of a young man named Antoine, a half-breed of French and Osage origin. He was to be a kind of Jack-of-all-work; to cook, to hunt, and to take care of the horses; but he had a vehement propensity to do nothing, being one of the worthless brood engendered and brought up among the missions. He was, moreover, a little spoiled by being really a handsome young fellow, an Adonis of the frontier, and still worse by fancying himself highly connected, his sister being concubine to an opulent white trader!

For our own parts, the commissioner and myself were desirous, before setting out, to procure another attendant well versed in woodcraft, who might serve us as a hunter; for our little Frenchman would have his hands full when in camp, in cooking, and on the march, in taking care of the pack-horses. Such a one presented himself, or rather was recommended to us, in Pierre Beatte, a half-breed of French and Osage parentage. We were assured that he was acquainted with all parts of the country, having traversed it in all directions, both in hunting and war parties; that he would be of use both as guide and interpreter, and that he was a first-rate hunter.

I confess I did not like his looks when he was first presented to me. He was lounging about, in an old hunting frock and metasses or leggings, of deer skin, soiled and greased, and almost japanned by constant use. He was apparently about thirty-six years of age, square and strongly built. His features were not bad, being shaped not unlike those of Napoleon, but sharpened up, with high Indian cheek bones. Perhaps the dusky greenish hue of his complexion aided his resemblance to an old bronze bust I had seen of the Emperor. He had, however, a sullen, saturnine expression, set off by a slouched woolen hat, and elf locks that hung about his ears.

Such was the appearance of the man, and his manners were equally unprepossessing He was cold and laconic; made no promises or professions; stated the terms he required for the services of himself and his horse, which we thought rather high, but showed no disposition to abate them, nor any anxiety to secure our employ. He had altogether more of the red than the white man in his composition; and, as I had been taught to look upon all half-breeds with distrust, as an uncertain and faithless race, I would gladly have dispensed with the services of Pierre Beatte. We had no time, however, to look out for any one more to our taste, and had to make an arrangement with him on the spot. He then set about making his preparations for the journey, promising to join us at our evening's encampment.

One thing was yet wanting to fit me out for the prairies —a thoroughly trustworthy steed: I was not yet mounted to my mind. The gray I had bought, though strong and serviceable, was rough. At the last moment I succeeded in getting an excellent animal; a dark bay; powerful, active, generous-spirited, and in capital condition. I mounted him with exultation, and transferred the silver gray to Tonish, who was in such ecstasies at finding himself so completely *en Cavalier* that I feared he might realize the ancient and well-known proverb of "a beggar on horseback."

CHAPTER FOUR

THE DEPARTURE

THE long-drawn notes of a bugle at length gave the signal for departure. The rangers filed off in a straggling line of march through the woods: we were soon on horseback and following on, but were detained by the irregularity of the pack-horses. They were unaccustomed to keep the line, and straggled from side to side among the thickets, in spite of all the pesting and bedeviling of Tonish; who, mounted on his gallant gray, with a long rifle on his shoulder, worried after them, bestowing a superabundance of dry blows and curses.

We soon, therefore, lost sight of our escort, but managed to keep on their track, thridding lofty forests and entangled thickets, and passing by Indian wigwams and negro huts, until toward dusk we arrived at a frontier farmhouse, owned by a settler of the name of Berryhill. It was situated on a hill, below which the rangers had encamped in a circular grove, on the margin of a stream. The master of the house received us civilly, but could offer us no accommodation, for sickness prevailed in his family. He appeared himself to be in no very thriving condition, for though bulky in frame he had a sallow, unhealthy complexion, and a whiffling double voice, shifting abruptly from a treble to a thorough-bass.

Finding his log house was a mere hospital, crowded with invalids, we ordered our tent to be pitched in the farmyard.

We had not been long encamped when our recently engaged attendant, Beatte, the Osage half-breed, made his appearance. He came mounted on one horse and leading another, which seemed to be well packed with supplies for the expedition. Beatte was evidently an "old soldier," as to the

art of taking care of himself and looking out for emergencies.
Finding that he was in government employ, being engaged
by the commissioner, he had drawn rations of flour and bacon,
and put them up so as to be weather-proof. In addition to
the horse for the road, and for ordinary service, which was
a rough, hardy animal, he had another for hunting. This
was of a mixed breed like himself, being a cross of the domestic stock with the wild horse of the prairies; and a noble
steed it was, of generous spirit, fine action, and admirable
bottom. He had taken care to have his horses well shod at
the Agency. He came prepared at all points for war or
hunting: his rifle on his shoulder, his powder-horn and bul-
let-pouch at his side, his hunting-knife stuck in his belt, and
coils of cordage at his saddle bow, which we were told were
lariats, or noosed cords, used in catching the wild horse.

Thus equipped and provided, an Indian hunter on a prairie
is like a cruiser on the ocean, perfectly independent of the
world, and competent to self-protection and self-maintenance.
He can cast himself loose from every one, shape his own
course, and take care of his own fortunes. I thought Beatte
seemed to feel his independence, and to consider himself superior to us all, now that we were launching into the wilderness. He maintained a half proud, half sullen look, and
great taciturnity, and his first care was to unpack his horses
and put them in safe quarters for the night. His whole demeanor was in perfect contrast to our vaporing, chattering,
bustling little Frenchman. The latter, too, seemed jealous
of this new-comer. He whispered to us that these half-
breeds were a touchy, capricious people, little to be depended
upon. That Beatte had evidently come prepared to take care
of himself, and that, at any moment in the course of our tour,
he would be liable to take some sudden disgust or affront,
and abandon us at a moment's warning; having the means
of shifting for himself, and being perfectly at home on the
prairies.

CHAPTER FIVE

FRONTIER SCENES—A LYCURGUS OF THE BORDER—LYNCH'S
LAW—THE DANGER OF FINDING A HORSE—THE
YOUNG OSAGE

ON the following morning (October 11), we were on the
march by half-past seven o'clock, and rode through deep
rich bottoms of alluvial soil, overgrown with redundant
vegetation, and trees of an enormous size. Our route lay
parallel to the west bank of the Arkansas, on the borders of
which river, near the confluence of the Red Fork, we expected to overtake the main body of rangers. For some
miles the country was sprinkled with Creek villages and
farmhouses; the inhabitants of which appeared to have
adopted, with considerable facility, the rudiments of civilization, and to have thriven in consequence. Their farms were
well stocked, and their houses had a look of comfort and
abundance.

We met with numbers of them returning from one of
their grand games of ball, for which their nation is cele-
brated. Some were on foot, some on horseback; the latter,
occasionally, with gayly dressed females behind them. They
are a well-made race, muscular and closely knit, with well-
turned thighs and legs. They have a gypsy fondness for
brilliant colors and gay decorations, and are bright and
fanciful objects when seen at a distance on the prairies. One
had a scarlet handkerchief bound round his head, surmounted
with a tuft of black feathers like a cocktail. Another had
a white handkerchief, with red feathers; while a third, for
want of a plume, had stuck in his turban a brilliant bunch of
sumach.

On the verge of the wilderness we paused to inquire our

way at a log house, owned by a white settler or squatter, a tall raw-boned old fellow, with red hair, a lank lantern visage, and an inveterate habit of winking with one eye, as if everything he said was of knowing import. He was in a towering passion. One of his horses was missing; he was sure it had been stolen in the night by a straggling party of Osages encamped in a neighboring swamp; but he would have satisfaction! He would make an example of the villains. He had accordingly caught down his rifle from the wall, that invariable enforcer of right or wrong upon the frontiers, and, having saddled his steed, was about to sally forth on a foray into the swamp; while a brother squatter, with rifle in hand, stood ready to accompany him.

We endeavored to calm the old campaigner of the prairies, by suggesting that his horse might have strayed into the neighboring woods; but he had the frontier propensity to charge everything to the Indians, and nothing could dissuade him from carrying fire and sword into the swamp.

After riding a few miles further we lost the trail of the main body of rangers, and became perplexed by a variety of tracks made by the Indians and settlers. At length coming to a log house, inhabited by a white man, the very last on the frontier, we found that we had wandered from our true course. Taking us back for some distance, he again brought us to the right trail; putting ourselves upon which, we took our final departure, and launched into the broad wilderness.

The trail kept on like a straggling footpath, over hill and dale, through brush and brake, and tangled thicket, and open prairie. In traversing the wilds it is customary for a party either of horse or foot to follow each other in single file like the Indians; so that the leaders break the way for those who follow, and lessen their labor and fatigue. In this way, also, the number of a party is concealed, the whole leaving but one narrow well-trampled track to mark their course.

We had not long regained the trail, when, on emerging from a forest, we beheld our raw-boned, hard-winking, hard-riding knight-errant of the frontier, descending the slope of a hill, followed by his companion in arms. As he drew near to us, the gauntness of his figure and ruefulness of his aspect reminded me of the description of the hero of La Mancha, and he was equally bent on affairs of doughty enterprise, being about to penetrate the thickets of the perilous swamp, within which the enemy lay ensconced.

While we were holding a parley with him on the slope of the hill, we descried an Osage on horseback issuing out of a skirt of wood about half a mile off, and leading a horse by a halter. The latter was immediately recognized by our hard-winking friend as the steed of which he was in quest. As the Osage drew near, I was struck with his appearance. He was about nineteen or twenty years of age, but well grown, with the fine Roman countenance common to his tribe, and as he rode with his blanket wrapped round his loins, his naked bust would have furnished a model for a statuary. He was mounted on a beautiful piebald horse, a mottled white and brown, of the wild breed of the prairies, decorated with a broad collar, from which hung in front a tuft of horse-hair dyed of a bright scarlet.

The youth rode slowly up to us with a frank open air, and signified, by means of our interpreter Beatte, that the horse he was leading had wandered to their camp, and he was now on his way to conduct him back to his owner.

I had expected to witness an expression of gratitude on the part of our hard-favored cavalier, but to my surprise the old fellow broke out into a furious passion. He declared that the Indians had carried off his horse in the night, with the intention of bringing him home in the morning, and claiming a reward for finding him; a common practice, as he affirmed, among the Indians. He was, therefore, for tying the young Indian to a tree and giving him a sound lashing; and was quite surprised at the burst of indignation which this novel mode of requiting a service drew from us. Such, however, is too often the administration of law on the frontier, "Lynch's law," as it is technically termed, in which
* * * 17—Vol. VII.

the plaintiff is apt to be witness, jury, judge, and execu-
tioner, and the defendant to be convicted and punished on
mere presumption; and in this way, I am convinced, are
occasioned many of those heart-burnings and resentments
among the Indians, which lead to retaliation, and end in
Indian wars. When I compared the open, noble countenance
and frank demeanor of the young Osage with the sinister
visage and high-handed conduct of the frontiersman, I felt
little doubt on whose back a lash would be most meritoriously
bestowed.

Being thus obliged to content himself with the recovery
of his horse, without the pleasure of flogging the finder into
the bargain, the old Lycurgus, or rather Draco, of the frontier, set off growling on his return homeward, followed by
his brother squatter.

As for the youthful Osage, we were all prepossessed in
his favor; the young count especially, with the sympathies
proper to his age and incident to his character, had taken
quite a fancy to him. Nothing would suit but he must have
the young Osage as a companion and squire in his expedition
into the wilderness. The youth was easily tempted, and,
with the prospect of a safe range over the buffalo prairies
and the promise of a new blanket, he turned his bridle, left
the swamp and the encampment of his friends behind him,
and set off to follow the count in his wanderings in quest of
the Osage hunters.

Such is the glorious independence of man in a savage
state. This youth, with his rifle, his blanket, and his horse,
was ready at a moment's warning to rove the world; he carried all his worldly effects with him, and in the absence of
artificial wants possessed the great secret of personal freedom. We of society are slaves, not so much to others as to
ourselves; our superfluities are the chains that bind us, im-
peding every movement of our bodies and thwarting every
impulse of our souls. Such, at least, were my speculations
at the time, though I am not sure but that they took their
tone from the enthusiasm of the young count, who seemed

more enchanted than ever with the wild chivalry of the prairies, and talked of putting on the Indian dress and adopting the Indian habits during the time he hoped to pass with the Osages.

CHAPTER SIX

TRAIL OF THE OSAGE HUNTERS—DEPARTURE OF THE COUNT AND HIS PARTY—A DESERTED WAR CAMP—A VAGRANT DOG—THE ENCAMPMENT

IN the course of the morning the trail we were pursuing was crossed by another, which struck off through the forest to the west in a direct course for the Arkansas River. Beatte, our half-breed, after considering it for a moment, pronounced it the trail of the Osage hunters; and that it must lead to the place where they had forded the river on their way to the hunting grounds.

Here then the young count and his companion came to a halt and prepared to take leave of us. The most experienced frontiersmen in the troop remonstrated on the hazard of the undertaking. They were about to throw themselves loose in the wilderness, with no other guides, guards, or attendants than a young ignorant half-breed and a still younger Indian. They were embarrassed by a pack-horse and two led horses, with which they would have to make their way through matted forests, and across rivers and morasses. The Osages and Pawnees were at war, and they might fall in with some warrior party of the latter, who are ferocious foes; besides, their small number, and their valuable horses, would form a great temptation to some of the straggling bands of Osages loitering about the frontier, who might rob them of their horses in the night, and leave them destitute and on foot in the midst of the prairies.

Nothing, however, could restrain the romantic ardor of the count for a campaign of buffalo hunting with the Osages,

and he had a game spirit that seemed always stimulated by
the idea of danger. His traveling companion, of discreeter
age and calmer temperament, was convinced of the rashness
of the enterprise; but he could not control the impetuous
zeal of his youthful friend, and he was too loyal to leave him
to pursue his hazardous scheme alone. To our great regret,
therefore, we saw them abandon the protection of our escort,
and strike off on their haphazard expedition. The old hunters of our party shook their heads, and our half-breed, Beatte,
predicted all kinds of trouble to them; my only hope was
that they would soon meet with perplexities enough to cool
the impetuosity of the young count and induce him to rejoin
us. With this idea we traveled slowly, and made a considerable halt at noon. After resuming our march, we came
in sight of the Arkansas. It presented a broad and rapid
stream, bordered by a beach of fine sand, overgrown with
willows and cotton-wood trees. Beyond the river, the eye
wandered over a beautiful champaign country, of flowery
plains and sloping uplands, diversified by groves and clumps
of trees, and long screens of woodland; the whole wearing
the aspect of complete and even ornamental cultivation, instead of native wildness. Not far from the river, on an open
eminence, we passed through the recently deserted camping
place of an Osage war party. The frames of the tents or
wigwams remained, consisting of poles bent into an arch,
with each end stuck into the ground; these are interwined
with twigs and branches, and covered with bark and skins.
Those experienced in Indian lore can ascertain the tribe, and
whether on a hunting or a warlike expedition, by the shape
and disposition of the wigwams. Beatte pointed out to us,
in the present skeleton camp, the wigwam in which the
chiefs had held their consultations around the council-fire;
and an open area, well trampled down, on which the grand
war-dance had been performed.

Pursuing our journey, as we were passing through a
forest we were met by a forlorn, half-famished dog, who
came rambling along the trail, with inflamed eyes and be-

wildered look. Though nearly trampled upon by the fore-most rangers, he took notice of no one, but rambled heed-lessly among the horses. The cry of "mad dog" was imme-diately raised, and one of the rangers leveled his rifle, but was stayed by the ever-ready humanity of the commissioner. "He is blind!" said he. "It is the dog of some poor Indian, following his master by the scent. It would be a shame to kill so faithful an animal." The ranger shouldered his rifle, the dog blundered blindly through the cavalcade unhurt, and, keeping his nose to the ground, continued his course along the trail, affording a rare instance of a dog surviving a bad name.

About three o'clock we came to a recent camping-place of the company of rangers: the brands of one of their fires were still smoking; so that, according to the opinion of Beatte, they could not have passed on above a day previ-ously. As there was a fine stream of water close by, and plenty of pea-vines for the horses, we encamped here for the night.

We had not been here long when we heard a halloo from a distance, and beheld the young count and his party ad-vancing through the forest. We welcomed them to the camp with heartfelt satisfaction; for their departure upon so hazardous an expedition had caused us great uneasiness. A short experiment had convinced them of the toil and diffi-culty of inexperienced travelers like themselves making their way through the wilderness with such a train of horses and such slender attendance. Fortunately, they determined to rejoin us before nightfall; one night's camping out might have cost them their horses. The count had prevailed upon his protege and esquire, the young Osage, to continue with him, and still calculated upon achieving great exploits, with his assistance, on the buffalo prairies.

CHAPTER SEVEN

NEWS OF THE RANGERS—THE COUNT AND HIS INDIAN SQUIRE
—HALT IN THE WOODS—WOODLAND SCENE—OSAGE VIL-
LAGE—OSAGE VISITORS AT OUR EVENING CAMP

IN the morning early (October 12th), the two Creeks who
had been sent express by the commander of Fort Gibson, to
stop the company of rangers, arrived at our encampment on
their return. They had left the company encamped about
fifty miles distant, in a fine place on the Arkansas, abounding in game, where they intended to await our arrival. This
news spread animation throughout our party, and we set out
on our march at sunrise with renewed spirit.

In mounting our steeds, the young Osage attempted to
throw a blanket upon his wild horse. The fine, sensible
animal took fright, reared and recoiled. The attitudes of
the wild horse and the almost naked savage would have
formed studies for a painter or a statuary.

I often pleased myself in the course of our march with
noticing the appearance of the young count and his newly
enlisted follower, as they rode before me. Never was preux
chevalier better suited with an esquire. The count was well
mounted, and, as I have before observed, was a bold and
graceful rider. He was fond, too, of caracoling his horse,
and dashing about in the buoyancy of youthful spirits. His
dress was a gay Indian hunting frock of dressed deer skin,
setting well to the shape, dyed of a beautiful purple, and
fancifully embroidered with silks of various colors; as if it
had been the work of some Indian beauty, to decorate a
favorite chief. With this he wore leathern pantaloons and
moccasins, a foraging cap, and a double-barreled gun slung
by a bandoleer athwart his back: so that he was quite a

picturesque figure as he managed gracefully his spirited steed.

The young Osage would ride close behind him on his wild and beautifully mottled horse, which was decorated with crimson tufts of hair. He rode with his finely shaped head and bust naked; his blanket being girt round his waist. He carried his rifle in one hand, and managed his horse with the other, and seemed ready to dash off at a moment's warning, with his youthful leader, on any madcap foray or scamper. The count, with the sanguine anticipations of youth, prom-ised himself many hardy adventures and exploits in company with his youthful "brave," when we should get among the buffaloes, in the Pawnee hunting grounds.

After riding some distance, we crossed a narrow, deep stream, upon a solid bridge, the remains of an old beaver dam; the industrious community which had constructed it had all been destroyed. Above us, a streaming flight of wild geese, high in the air, and making a vociferous noise, gave note of the waning year.

About half-past ten o'clock we made a halt in a forest, where there was abundance of the pea-vine. Here we turned the horses loose to graze. A fire was made, water procured from an adjacent spring, and in a short time our little French-man, Tonish, had a pot of coffee prepared for our refresh-ment. While partaking of it, we were joined by an old Osage, one of a small hunting party who had recently passed this way. He was in search of his horse, which had wan-dered away or been stolen. Our half-breed, Beatte, made a wry face on hearing of Osage hunters in this direction. "Until we pass those hunters," said he, "we shall see no buffaloes. They frighten away everything, like a prairie on fire."

The morning repast being over, the party amused them-selves in various ways. Some shot with their rifles at a mark, others lay asleep half buried in the deep bed of foliage, with their heads resting on their saddles; others gossiped round the fire at the foot of a tree, which sent up wreaths

of blue smoke among the branches. The horses banqueted
luxuriously on the pea-vines, and some lay down and rolled
among them.

We were overshadowed by lofty trees, with straight,
smooth trunks, like stately columns; and as the glancing
rays of the sun shone through the transparent leaves, tinted
with the many-colored hues of autumn, I was reminded of
the effect of sunshine among the stained windows and clus-
tering columns of a Gothic cathedral. Indeed there is a
grandeur and solemnity in our spacious forests of the West
that awaken in me the same feeling I have experienced in
those vast and venerable piles, and the sound of the wind
sweeping through them supplies occasionally the deep
breathings of the organ.

About noon the bugle sounded to horse, and we were
again on the march, hoping to arrive at the encampment of
the rangers before night; as the old Osage had assured us it
was not above ten or twelve miles distant. In our course
through a forest we passed by a lonely pool, covered with
the most magnificent water-lilies I had ever beheld; among
which swam several wood-ducks, one of the most beautiful
of water-fowl, remarkable for the gracefulness and brilliancy
of its plumage.

After proceeding some distance further, we came down
upon the banks of the Arkansas, at a place where tracks of
numerous horses, all entering the water, showed where a
party of Osage hunters had recently crossed the river on
their way to the buffalo range. After letting our horses
drink in the river, we continued along its bank for a space,
and then across prairies, where we saw a distant smoke,
which we hoped might proceed from the encampment of the
rangers. Following what we supposed to be their trail, we
came to a meadow in which were a number of horses grazing: they were not, however, the horses of the troop. A
little further on, we reached a straggling Osage village, on
the banks of the Arkansas. Our arrival created quite a
sensation. A number of old men came forward and shook

hands with us all severally; while the women and children huddled together in groups, staring at us wildly, chattering and laughing among themselves. We found that all the young men of the village had departed on a hunting expedition, leaving the women and children and old men behind. Here the commissioner made a speech from on horseback; informing his hearers of the purport of his mission, to promote a general peace among the tribes of the West, and urging them to lay aside all warlike and bloodthirsty notions, and not to make any wanton attacks upon the Pawnees. This speech being interpreted by Beatte, seemed to have a most pacifying effect upon the multitude, who promised faithfully that, as far as in them lay, the peace should not be disturbed; and indeed their age and sex gave some reason to trust that they would keep their word.

Still hoping to reach the camp of the rangers before nightfall, we pushed on until twilight, when we were obliged to halt on the borders of a ravine. The rangers bivouacked under trees, at the bottom of the dell, while we pitched our tent on a rocky knoll near a running stream. The night came on dark and overcast, with flying clouds, and much appearance of rain. The fires of the rangers burned brightly in the dell, and threw strong masses of light upon the robber-looking groups that were cooking, eating, and drinking around them. To add to the wildness of the scene, several Osage Indians, visitors from the village we had passed, were mingled among the men. Three of them came and seated themselves by our fire. They watched everything that was going on around them in silence, and looked like figures of monumental bronze. We gave them food, and, what they most relished, coffee; for the Indians partake in the universal fondness for this beverage, which pervades the West. When they had made their supper, they stretched themselves, side by side, before the fire, and began a low nasal chant, drumming with their hands upon their breasts, by way of accompaniment. Their chant seemed to consist of regular staves, every one terminating, not in a melodious cadence, but in the abrupt interjection huh! uttered almost like a hiccup. This chant, we were told by our interpreter, Beatte, related to ourselves, our appearance, our treatment of them, and all that they knew of our plans. In one part they spoke of the young count, whose animated character and eagerness for Indian enterprise had struck their fancy, and they indulged in some waggery about him and the young Indian beauties, that produced great merriment among our half-breeds.

This mode of improvising is common throughout the savage tribes; and in this way, with a few simple inflections of the voice, they chant all their exploits in war and hunting, and occasionally indulge in a vein of comic humor and dry satire, to which the Indians appear to me much more prone than is generally imagined.

In fact, the Indians that I have had an opportunity of seeing in real life are quite different from those described in poetry. They are by no means the stoics that they are represented; taciturn, unbending, without a tear or a smile. Taciturn they are, it is true, when in company with white men, whose good-will they distrust, and whose language they do not understand; but the white man is equally taciturn under like circumstances. When the Indians are among themselves, however, there cannot be greater gossips. Half their time is taken up in talking over their adventures in war and hunting, and in telling whimsical stories. They are great mimics and buffoons, also, and entertain themselves excessively at the expense of the whites with whom they have associated, and who have supposed them impressed with profound respect for their grandeur and dignity. They are curious observers, noting everything in silence, but with a keen and watchful eye; occasionally exchanging a glance or a grunt with each other, when anything particularly strikes them: but reserving all comments until they are alone. Then it is that they give full scope to criticism, satire, mimicry, and mirth.

In the course of my journey along the frontier, I have had repeated opportunities of noticing their excitability and boisterous merriment at their games; and have occasionally noticed a group of Osages sitting round a fire until a late hour of the night, engaged in the most animated and lively conversation; and at times making the woods resound with peals of laughter. As to tears, they have them in abundance, both real and affected; at times they make a merit of them. No one weeps more bitterly or profusely at the death of a relative or friend; and they have stated times when they repair to howl and lament at their graves. I have heard doleful wailings at daybreak, in the neighboring Indian villages, made by some of the inhabitants, who go out at that hour into the fields, to mourn and weep for the dead: at such times, I am told, the tears will stream down their cheeks in torrents.

As far as I can judge, the Indian of poetical fiction is like the shepherd of pastoral romance, a mere personification of imaginary attributes.

The nasal chant of our Osage guests gradually died away; they covered their heads with their blankets and fell fast asleep, and in a little while all was silent, excepting the pattering of scattered rain drops upon our tent.

In the morning our Indian visitors breakfasted with us, but the young Osage who was to act as esquire to the count in his knight-errantry on the prairies was nowhere to be found. His wild horse, too, was missing, and, after many conjectures, we came to the conclusion that he had taken "Indian leave" of us in the night. We afterward ascertained that he had been persuaded so to do by the Osages we had recently met with; who had represented to him the perils that would attend him in an expedition to the Pawnee hunting grounds, where he might fall into the hands of the implacable enemies of his tribe; and, what was scarcely less to be apprehended, the annoyances to which he would be subjected from the capricious and overbearing conduct of the white men; who, as I have witnessed in my own short experience, are prone to treat the poor Indians as little better than brute animals. Indeed, he had had a specimen of it

himself in the narrow escape he made from the infliction of
"Lynch's law," by the hard-winking worthy of the frontier,
for the flagitious crime of finding a stray horse.

The disappearance of the youth was generally regretted
by our party, for we had all taken a great fancy to him from
his handsome, frank, and manly appearance, and the easy
grace of his deportment. He was indeed a native-born gentleman. By none, however, was he so much lamented as by
the young count, who thus suddenly found himself deprived
of his esquire. I regretted the departure of the Osage for
his own sake, for we should have cherished him throughout
the expedition, and I am convinced, from the munificent
spirit of his patron, he would have returned to his tribe laden
with wealth of beads and trinkets and Indian blankets.

CHAPTER EIGHT

THE HONEY CAMP

THE weather, which had been rainy in the night, having
held up, we resumed our march at seven o'clock in the morning, in confident hope of soon arriving at the encampment of
the rangers. We had not ridden above three or four miles
when we came to a large tree which had recently been felled
by an ax, for the wild honey contained in the hollow of its
trunk, several broken flakes of which still remained. We
now felt sure that the camp could not be far distant. About
a couple of miles further some of the rangers set up a shout,
and pointed to a number of horses grazing in a woody bottom. A few paces brought us to the brow of an elevated
ridge, whence we looked down upon the encampment. It
was a wild bandit, or Robin Hood, scene. In a beautiful
open forest, traversed by a running stream, were booths of
bark and branches, and tents of blankets, temporary shelters
from the recent rain, for the rangers commonly bivouac in

the open air. There were groups of rangers in every kind
of uncouth garb. Some were cooking at large fires made at
the feet of trees; some were stretching and dressing deer
skins; some were shooting at a mark, and some lying about
on the grass. Venison jerked, and hung on frames, was
drying over the embers in one place; in another lay carcasses
recently brought in by the hunters. Stacks of rifles were
leaning against the trunks of the trees, and saddles, bridles,
and powder-horns hanging above them, while the horses
were grazing here and there among the thickets.

Our arrival was greeted with acclamation. The rangers
crowded about their comrades to inquire the news from the
fort; for our own part, we were received in frank simple
hunter's style by Captain Bean, the commander of the company; a man about forty years of age, vigorous and active.
His life had been chiefly passed on the frontier, occasionally
in Indian warfare, so that he was a thorough woodsman, and
a first-rate hunter. He was equipped in character; in leathern hunting shirt and leggings, and a leathern foraging cap.

While we were conversing with the captain, a veteran
huntsman approached, whose whole appearance struck me.
He was of the middle size, but tough and weather-proved; a
head partly bald and garnished with loose iron-gray locks,
and a fine black eye, beaming with youthful spirit. His
dress was similar to that of the captain, a rifle shirt and leggings of dressed deer skin, that had evidently seen service;
a powder-horn was slung by his side, a hunting-knife stuck
in his belt, and in his hand was an ancient and trusty rifle,
doubtless as dear to him as a bosom friend. He asked permission to go hunting, which was readily granted. "That's
old Ryan," said the captain, when he had gone; "there's
not a better hunter in the camp; he's sure to bring in game."

In a little while our pack-horses were unloaded and turned
loose to revel among the pea-vines. Our tent was pitched;
our fire made; the half of a deer had been sent to us from
the captain's lodge; Beatte brought in a couple of wild turkeys; the spits were laden, and the camp kettle crammed

with meat; and to crown our luxuries, a basin filled with great flakes of delicious honey, the spoils of a plundered bee-tree, was given us by one of the rangers.

Our little Frenchman, Tonish, was in an ecstasy, and tucking up his sleeves to the elbows, set to work to make a display of his culinary skill, on which he prided himself almost as much as upon his hunting, his riding, and his warlike prowess.

CHAPTER NINE

A BEE HUNT

THE beautiful forest in which we were encamped abounded in bee-trees; that is to say, trees in the decayed trunks of which wild bees had established their hives. It is surprising in what countless swarms the bees have overspread the Far West, within but a moderate number of years. The Indians consider them the harbinger of the white man, as the buffalo is of the red man; and say that, in proportion as the bee advances, the Indian and buffalo retire. We are always accustomed to associate the hum of the bee-hive with the farmhouse and flower-garden, and to consider those indus-trious little animals as connected with the busy haunts of man, and I am told that the wild bee is seldom to be met with at any great distance from the frontier. They have been the heralds of civilization, steadfastly preceding it as it advanced from the Atlantic borders, and some of the ancient settlers of the West pretend to give the very year when the honey-bee first crossed the Mississippi. The Indians with surprise found the mouldering trees of their forests suddenly teeming with ambrosial sweets, and nothing, I am told, can exceed the greedy relish with which they banquet for the first time upon this unbought luxury of the wilderness.

At present the honey-bee swarms in myriads, in the noble groves and forests which skirt and intersect the prairies, and extend along the alluvial bottoms of the rivers. It seems to me as if these beautiful regions answer literally to the description of the land of promise, "a land flowing with milk and honey"; for the rich pasturage of the prairies is calculated to sustain herds of cattle as countless as the sands upon the seashore, while the flowers with which they are enameled render them a very paradise for the nectar-seeking bee.

We had not been long in the camp when a party set out in quest of a bee-tree; and, being curious to witness the sport, I gladly accepted an invitation to accompany them. The party was headed by a veteran bee-hunter, a tall lank fellow in homespun garb that hung loosely about his limbs, and a straw hat shaped not unlike a bee-hive; a comrade, equally uncouth in garb, and without a hat, straddled along at his heels, with a long rifle on his shoulder. To these succeeded half a dozen others, some with axes and some with rifles, for no one stirs far from the camp without his firearms, so as to be ready either for wild deer or wild Indian.

After proceeding some distance we came to an open glade on the skirts of the forest. Here our leader halted, and then advanced quietly to a low bush, on the top of which I perceived a piece of honey-comb. This I found was the bait or lure for the wild bees. Several were humming about it, and diving into its cells. When they had laden themselves with honey they would rise into the air, and dart off in a straight line, almost with the velocity of a bullet. The hunters watched attentively the course they took, and then set off in the same direction, stumbling along over twisted roots and fallen trees, with their eyes turned up to the sky. In this way they traced the honey-laden bees to their hive, in the hollow trunk of a blasted oak, where, after buzzing about for a moment, they entered a hole about sixty feet from the ground.

Two of the bee-hunters now plied their axes vigorously at the foot of the tree to level it with the ground. The mere spectators and amateurs, in the meantime, drew off to a cautious distance, to be out of the way of the falling of the tree and the vengeance of its inmates. The jarring blows of the

ax seemed to have no effect in alarming or disturbing this
most industrious community. They continued to ply at their
usual occupations, some arriving full freighted into port,
others sallying forth on new expeditions, like so many mer-
chantmen in a money-making metropolis, little suspicious of
impending bankruptcy and downfall. Even a loud crack
which announced the disrupture of the trunk failed to divert
their attention from the intense pursuit of gain; at length
down came the tree with a tremendous crash, bursting open
from end to end, and displaying all the hoarded treasures of
the commonwealth.

One of the hunters immediately ran up with a wisp of
lighted hay as a defense against the bees. The latter, however, made no attack and sought no revenge; they seemed
stupefied by the catastrophe and unsuspicious of its cause,
and remained crawling and buzzing about the ruins without
offering us any molestation. Every one of the party now
fell to, with spoon and hunting-knife, to scoop out the flakes
of honeycomb with which the hollow trunk was stored.
Some of them were of old date and a deep brown color,
others were beautifully white, and the honey in their cells
was almost limpid. Such of the combs as were entire were
placed in camp kettles to be conveyed to the encampment;
those which had been shivered in the fall were devoured
upon the spot. Every stark bee-hunter was to be seen with
a rich morsel in his hand, dripping about his fingers, and
disappearing as rapidly as a cream tart before the holiday
appetite of a schoolboy.

Nor was it the bee-hunters alone that profited by the
downfall of this industrious community; as if the bees would
carry through the similitude of their habits with those of
laborious and gainful man, I beheld numbers from rival
hives, arriving on eager wing, to enrich themselves with the
ruins of their neighbors. These busied themselves as eagerly
and cheerfully as so many wreckers on an Indiaman that has
been driven on shore; plunging into the cells of the broken
honeycombs, banqueting greedily on the spoil, and then wing-

ing their way full-freighted to their homes. As to the poor proprietors of the ruin, they seemed to have no heart to do anything, not even to taste the nectar that flowed around them; but crawled backward and forward, in vacant desolation, as I have seen a poor fellow with his hands in his pockets, whistling vacantly and despondingly about the ruins of his house that had been burned.

It is difficult to describe the bewilderment and confusion of the bees of the bankrupt hive who had been absent at the time of the catastrophe, and who arrived from time to time, with full cargoes from abroad. At first they wheeled about in the air, in the place where the fallen tree had once reared its head, astonished at finding it all a vacuum. At length, as if comprehending their disaster, they settled down in clusters on a dry branch of a neighboring tree, whence they seemed to contemplate the prostrate ruin, and to buzz forth doleful lamentations over the downfall of their republic. It was a scene on which the "melancholy Jacques" might have moralized by the hour.

We now abandoned the place, leaving much honey in the hollow of the tree. "It will all be cleared off by varmint," said one of the rangers. "What vermin?" asked I. "Oh, bears, and skunks, and raccoons, and 'possums. The bears is the knowingest varmint for finding out a bee-tree in the world. They'll gnaw for days together at the trunk till they make a hole big enough to get in their paws, and then they'll haul out honey, bees and all."

CHAPTER TEN

AMUSEMENTS IN THE CAMP — CONSULTATIONS — HUNTERS' FARE AND FEASTING—EVENING SCENES—CAMP MELODY —THE FATE OF AN AMATEUR OWL

ON returning to the camp, we found it a scene of the greatest hilarity. Some of the rangers were shooting at a mark.

others were leaping, wrestling, and playing at prison bars. They were mostly young men, on their first expedition, in high health and vigor, and buoyant with anticipations; and I can conceive nothing more likely to set the youthful blood into flow than a wild wood life of the kind, and the range of a magnificent wilderness, abounding with game and fruitful of adventure. We send our youth abroad to grow luxurious and effeminate in Europe; it appears to me that a previous tour on the prairies would be more likely to produce that manliness, simplicity, and self-dependence most in unison with our political institutions.

While the young men were engaged in these boisterous amusements, a graver set, composed of the captain, the doctor, and other sages and leaders of the camp, were seated or stretched out on the grass, round a frontier map, holding a consultation about our position and the course we were to pursue.

Our plan was to cross the Arkansas just above where the Red Fork falls into it, then to keep westerly, until we should pass through a grand belt of open forest, called the Cross Timber, which ranges nearly north and south from the Arkansas to Red River; after which we were to keep a southerly course toward the latter river.

Our half-breed, Beatte, being an experienced Osage hunter, was called into the consultation. "Have you ever hunted in this direction?" said the captain.

"Yes," was the laconic reply.

"Perhaps, then, you can tell us in which direction lies the Red Fork?"

"If you keep along yonder, by the edge of the prairie, you will come to a bald hill, with a pile of stones upon it."

"I have noticed that hill as I was hunting," said the captain.

"Well! those stones were set up by the Osages as a landmark: from that spot you may have a sight of the Red Fork."

"In that case," cried the captain, "we shall reach the Red Fork to-morrow; then cross the Arkansas above it, into the

Pawnee country, and then in two days we shall crack buffalo
bones!''

The idea of arriving at the adventurous hunting grounds
of the Pawnees, and of coming upon the traces of the buffaloes, made very eye sparkle with animation. Our further
conversation was interrupted by the sharp report of a rifle at
no great distance from the camp.

''That's old Ryan's rifle,'' exclaimed the captain; ''there's
a buck down, I'll warrant!'' Nor was he mistaken; for, before long, the veteran made his appearance, calling upon one
of the younger rangers to return with him, and aid in bringing home the carcass.

The surrounding country, in fact, abounded with game,
so that the camp was overstocked with provisions, and, as no
less than twenty bee-trees had been cut down in the vicinity,
every one reveled in luxury. With the wasteful prodigality
of hunters, there was a continual feasting, and scarce any
one put by provision for the morrow. The cooking was conducted in hunter's style: the meat was stuck upon tapering
spits of dogwood, which were thrust perpendicularly into the
ground, so as to sustain the joint before the fire, where it was
roasted or broiled with all its juices retained in it in a manner that would have tickled the palate of the most experienced gourmand. As much could not be said in favor of
the bread. It was little more than a paste made of flour and
water, and fried like fritters, in lard; though some adopted
a ruder style, twisting it round the ends of sticks, and thus
roasting it before the fire. In either way, I have found it
extremely palatable on the prairies. No one knows the true
relish of food until he has a hunter's appetite.

Before sunset, we were summoned by little Tonish to a
sumptuous repast. Blankets had been spread on the ground
near to the fire, upon which we took our seats. A large dish,
or bowl, made from the root of a maple tree, and which we
had purchased at the Indian village, was placed on the ground
before us, and into it were emptied the contents of one of the
camp kettles, consisting of a wild turkey hashed, together

with slices of bacon and lumps of dough. Beside it was placed another bowl of similar ware, containing an ample supply of fritters. After we had discussed the hash, two wooden spits, on which the ribs of a fat buck were broiling before the fire, were removed and planted in the ground before us, with a triumphant air, by little Tonish. Having no dishes, we had to proceed in hunter's style, cutting off strips and slices with our hunting-knives, and dipping them in salt and pepper. To do justice to Tonish's cookery, however, and to the keen sauce of the prairies, never have I tasted venison so delicious. With all this, our beverage was coffee, boiled in a camp kettle, sweetened with brown sugar, and drunk out of tin cups: and such was the style of our banqueting throughout this expedition, whenever provisions were plenty, and as long as flour and coffee and sugar held out.

As the twilight thickened into night, the sentinels were marched forth to their stations around the camp; an indispensable precaution in a country infested by Indians. The encampment now presented a picturesque appearance. Camp fires were blazing and smoldering here and there among the trees, with groups of rangers round them; some seated or lying on the ground, others standing in the ruddy glare of the flames, or in shadowy relief. At some of the fires there was much boisterous mirth, where peals of laughter were mingled with loud ribald jokes and uncouth exclamations; for the troop was evidently a raw, undisciplined band, levied among the wild youngsters of the frontier, who had enlisted, some for the sake of roving adventure, and some for the purpose of getting a knowledge of the country. Many of them were the neighbors of their officers, and accustomed to regard them with the familiarity of equals and companions. None of them had any idea of the restraint and decorum of a camp, or ambition to acquire a name for exactness in a profession in which they had no intention of continuing.

While this boisterous merriment prevailed at some of the fires, there suddenly rose a strain of nasal melody from another, at which a choir of "vocalists" were uniting their voices

in a most lugubrious psalm tune. This was led by one of the
lieutenants; a tall, spare man, who we were informed had
officiated as schoolmaster, singing-master, and occasionally
as Methodist preacher, in one of the villages of the frontier.
The chant rose solemnly and sadly in the night air, and reminded me of the description of similar canticles in the camps
of the Covenanters; and, indeed, the strange medley of figures and faces and uncouth garbs, congregated together in
our troop, would not have disgraced the banners of Praise-
God Barebones.

In one of the intervals of this nasal psalmody, an amateur
owl, as if in competition, began his dreary hooting. Immediately there was a cry throughout the camp of "Charley's
owl! Charley's owl!" It seems this "obscure bird" had
visited the camp every night, and had been fired at by one
of the sentinels, a half-witted lad named Charley; who, on
being called up for firing when on duty, excused himself by
saying that he understood owls made uncommonly good
soup.

One of the young rangers mimicked the cry of this bird of
wisdom, who, with a simplicity little consonant with his character, came hovering within sight, and alighted on the naked
branch of a tree, lighted up by the blaze of our fire. The
young count immediately seized his fowling-piece, took fatal
aim, and in a twinkling the poor bird of ill-omen came fluttering to the ground. Charley was now called upon to make
and eat his dish of owl-soup, but declined, as he had not shot
the bird.

In the course of the evening, I paid a visit to the captain's
fire. It was composed of huge trunks of trees, and of sufficient magnitude to roast a buffalo whole. Here were a number of the prime hunters and leaders of the camp, some sitting, some standing, and others lying on skins or blankets
before the fire, telling old frontier stories about hunting and
Indian warfare.

As the night advanced, we perceived above the trees to
the west a ruddy glow flushing up the sky.

"That must be a prairie set on fire by the Osage hunters," said the captain.

"It is at the Red Fork," said Beatte, regarding the sky. "It seems but three miles distant, yet it perhaps is twenty."

About half-past eight o'clock, a beautiful pale light gradually sprang up in the east, a precursor of the rising moon. Drawing off from the captain's lodge, I now prepared for the night's repose. I had determined to abandon the shelter of the tent, and henceforth to bivouac like the rangers. A bear-skin spread at the foot of a tree was my bed, with a pair of saddle-bags for a pillow. Wrapping myself in blankets, I stretched myself on this hunter's couch, and soon fell into a sound and sweet sleep, from which I did not awake until the bugle sounded at daybreak.

CHAPTER ELEVEN

BREAKING UP OF THE ENCAMPMENT—PICTURESQUE MARCH —GAME—CAMP SCENES—TRIUMPH OF A YOUNG HUNTER —ILL SUCCESS OF AN OLD HUNTER—FOUL MURDER OF A POLECAT

OCTOBER 14TH.—At the signal-note of the bugle the sentinels and patrols marched in from their stations around the camp and were dismissed. The rangers were roused from their night's repose, and soon a bustling scene took place. While some cut wood, made fires, and prepared the morning's meal, others struck their foul-weather shelters of blankets, and made every preparation for departure; while others dashed about, through brush and brake, catching the horses and leading or driving them into camp.

During all this bustle the forest rang with whoops and shouts, and peals of laughter; when all had breakfasted, packed up their effects and camp equipage, and loaded the pack-horses, the bugle sounded to saddle and mount. By eight o'clock the whole troop set off in a long straggling line,

with whoop and halloo, intermingled with many an oath at
the loitering pack-horses, and in a little while the forest,
which for several days had been the scene of such unwonted
bustle and uproar, relapsed into its primeval solitude and
silence.

It was a bright sunny morning, with a pure transparent
atmosphere that seemed to bathe the very heart with glad-
ness.   Our march continued parallel to the Arkansas, through
a rich and varied country; sometimes we had to break our
way through alluvial bottoms matted with redundant vegetation, where the gigantic trees were entangled with grapevines, hanging like cordage from their branches; sometimes
we coasted along sluggish brooks, whose feebly trickling current just served to link together a succession of glassy pools,
imbedded like mirrors in the quiet bosom of the forest, re-
flecting its autumnal foliage and patches of the clear blue
sky.   Sometimes we scrambled up broken and rocky hills,
from the summits of which we had wide views stretching on
one side over distant prairies diversified by groves and forests, and on the other ranging along a line of blue and
shadowy hills beyond the waters of the Arkansas.

The appearance of our troop was suited to the country;
stretching along in a line of upward of half a mile in length,
winding among brakes and bushes, and up and down in the
defiles of the hills, the men in every kind of uncouth garb,
with long rifles on their shoulders, and mounted on horses of
every color.   The pack-horses, too, would incessantly wander from the line of march, to crop the surrounding herbage,
and were banged and beaten back by Tonish and his half-
breed compeers, with volleys of mongrel oaths.   Every now
and then the notes of the bugle, from the head of the column, would echo through the woodlands and along the hollow glens, summoning up stragglers, and announcing the
line of march.   The whole scene reminded me of the description given of bands of buccaneers penetrating the wilds
of South America, on their plundering expeditions against
the Spanish settlements.

At one time we passed through a luxuriant bottom or meadow bordered by thickets, where the tall grass was pressed down into numerous "deer beds," where those animals had couched the preceding night. Some oak trees also bore signs of having been clambered by bears, in quest of acorns, the marks of their claws being visible in the bark.

As we opened a glade of this sheltered meadow we beheld several deer bounding away in wild affright, until, having gained some distance, they would stop and gaze back, with the curiosity common to this animal, at the strange intruders into their solitudes. There was immediately a sharp report of rifles in every direction, from the young huntsmen of the troop, but they were too eager to aim surely, and the deer, unharmed, bounded away into the depths of the forest.

In the course of our march we struck the Arkansas, but found ourselves still below the Red Fork, and, as the river made deep bends, we again left its banks and continued through the woods until nearly eight o'clock, when we encamped in a beautiful basin bordered by a fine stream, and shaded by clumps of lofty oaks.

The horses were now hobbled, that is to say, their forelegs were fettered with cords or leathern straps, so as to impede their movements and prevent their wandering from the camp. They were then turned loose to graze. A number of rangers, prime hunters, started off in different directions in search of game. There was no whooping nor laughing about the camp as in the morning; all were either busy about the fires preparing the evening's repast or reposing upon the grass. Shots were soon heard in various directions. After a time a huntsman rode into the camp with the carcass of a fine buck hanging across his horse. Shortly afterward came in a couple of stripling hunters on foot, one of whom bore on his shoulders the body of a doe. He was evidently proud of his spoil, being probably one of his first achievements, though he and his companion were much bantered by their comrades, as young beginners who hunted in partnership.

Just as the night set in, there was a great shouting at one

end of the camp, and immediately afterward a body of young rangers came parading round the various fires, bearing one of their comrades in triumph on their shoulders. He had shot an elk for the first time in his life, and it was the first animal of the kind that had been killed on this expedition. The young huntsman, whose name was M'Lellan, was the hero of the camp for the night, and was the "father of the feast" into the bargain; for portions of his elk were seen roasting at every fire.

The other hunters returned without success. The captain had observed the tracks of a buffalo, which must have passed within a few days, and had tracked a bear for some distance until the footprints had disappeared. He had seen an elk, too, on the banks of the Arkansas, which walked out on a sand-bar of the river, but before he could steal round through the bushes to get a shot it had re-entered the woods.

Our own hunter, Beatte, returned silent and sulky, from an unsuccessful hunt. As yet he had brought us in nothing, and we had depended for our supplies of venison upon the captain's mess. Beatte was evidently mortified, for he looked down with contempt upon the rangers, as raw and inexperienced woodsmen, but little skilled in hunting; they, on the other hand, regarded Beatte with no very complacent eye, as one of an evil breed, and always spoke of him as "the Indian."

Our little Frenchman, Tonish, also, by his incessant boasting, and chattering, and gasconading, in his balderdashed dialect, had drawn upon himself the ridicule of many of the wags of the troop, who amused themselves at his expense in a kind of raillery by no means remarkable for its delicacy; but the little varlet was so completely fortified by vanity and self-conceit that he was invulnerable to every joke. I must confess, however, that I felt a little mortified at the sorry figure our retainers were making among these moss-troopers of the frontier. Even our very equipments came in for a share of unpopularity, and I heard many sneers at the double-barreled guns with which we were provided against smaller game; the lads of the West holding "shotguns," as they call them, in great contempt, thinking grouse, partridges, and even wild turkeys as beneath their serious attention, and the rifle the only firearm worthy of a hunter.

I was awakened before daybreak the next morning by the mournful howling of a wolf, who was skulking about the purlieus of the camp, attracted by the scent of venison. Scarcely had the first gray streak of dawn appeared, when a youngster at one of the distant lodges, shaking off his sleep, crowed in imitation of a cock, with a loud clear note and prolonged cadence that would have done credit to the most veteran chanticleer. He was immediately answered from another quarter, as if from a rival rooster. The chant was echoed from lodge to lodge, and followed by the cackling of hens, quacking of ducks, gabbling of turkeys, and grunting of swine, until we seemed to have been transported into the midst of a farmyard, with all its inmates in full concert around us.

After riding a short distance this morning, we came upon a well-worn Indian track, and following it, scrambled to the summit of a hill, whence we had a wide prospect over a country diversified by rocky ridges and waving lines of upland, and enriched by groves and clumps of trees of varied tuft and foliage. At a distance to the west, to our great satisfaction, we beheld the Red Fork rolling its ruddy current to the Arkansas, and found that we were above the point of junction. We now descended and pushed forward, with much difficulty, through the rich alluvial bottom that borders the Arkansas. Here the trees were interwoven with grapevines, forming a kind of cordage, from trunk to trunk and limb to limb; there was a thick undergrowth, also, of bush and bram·ble, and such an abundance of hops, fit for gathering, that it was difficult for our horses to force their way through.

The soil was imprinted in many places with the tracks of deer, and the claws of bears were to be traced on various trees. Every one was on the lookout in the hope of starting some game, when suddenly there was a bustle and a clamor in a distant part of the line. A bear! a bear! was the cry. We all pressed forward to be present at the sport, when to my infinite, though whimsical chagrin, I found it to be our two worthies, Beatte and Tonish, perpetrating a foul murder on a polecat or skunk! The animal had ensconced itself beneath the trunk of a fallen tree, whence it kept up a vigorous defense in its peculiar style, until the surrounding forest was in a high state of fragrance.

Gibes and jokes now broke out on all sides at the expense of the Indian hunter, and he was advised to wear the scalp of the skunk as the only trophy of his prowess. When they found, however, that he and Tonish were absolutely bent upon bearing off the carcass as a peculiar dainty, there was a universal expression of disgust; and they were regarded as little better than cannibals.

Mortified at this ignominious debut of our two hunters I insisted upon their abandoning their prize and resuming their march. Beatte complied with a dogged, discontented air, and lagged behind muttering to himself. Tonish, however, with his usual buoyancy, consoled himself by vociferous eulogies on the richness and delicacy of a roasted polecat, which he swore was considered the daintiest of dishes by all experienced Indian gourmands. It was with difficulty I could silence his loquacity by repeated and peremptory commands. A Frenchman's vivacity, however, if repressed in one way, will break out in another, and Tonish now eased off his spleen by bestowing volleys of oaths and dry blows on the packhorses. I was likely to be no gainer in the end by my opposition to the humors of these varlets, for after a time, Beatte, who had lagged behind, rode up to the head of the line to resume his station as a guide, and I had the vexation to see the carcass of his prize, stripped of its skin, and looking like a fat sucking-pig, dangling behind his saddle. I made a solemn vow, however, in secret, that our fire should not be disgraced by the cooking of that polecat.

CHAPTER TWELVE

THE CROSSING OF THE ARKANSAS

WE had now arrived at the river, about a quarter of a mile above the junction of the Red Fork; but the banks were steep and crumbling, and the current was deep and rapid. It was impossible, therefore, to cross at this place; and we resumed our painful course through the forest, dispatching Beatte ahead in search of a fording place. We had proceeded about a mile further, when he rejoined us, bringing intelligence of a place hard by, where the river, for a great part of its breadth, was rendered fordable by sand-bars, and the remainder might easily be swum by the horses.

Here, then, we made a halt. Some of the rangers set to work vigorously with their axes, felling trees on the edge of the river, wherewith to form rafts for the transportation of their baggage and camp equipage. Others patroled the banks of the river further up, in hopes of finding a better fording place; being unwilling to risk their horses in the deep channel.

It was now that our worthies, Beatte and Tonish, had an opportunity of displaying their Indian adroitness and resource. At the Osage village which we had passed a day or two before, they had procured a dry buffalo skin. This was now produced; cords were passed through a number of small eyelet-holes with which it was bordered, and it was drawn up, until it formed a kind of deep trough. Sticks were then placed athwart it on the inside, to keep it in shape; our camp equipage and a part of our baggage were placed within, and the singular bark was carried down the bank and set afloat. A cord was attached to the prow, which Beatte took between his teeth, and throwing himself into the water, went ahead, towing the bark after him; while Tonish followed behind, to keep it steady and to propel it. Part of the way they had foothold, and were enabled to wade, but in the main current they were obliged to swim. The whole way, they whooped and yelled in the Indian style, until they landed safely on the opposite shore.

The commissioner and myself were so well pleased with this Indian mode of ferriage that we determined to trust ourselves in the buffalo hide. Our companions, the count and Mr. L., had proceeded with the horses, along the river bank, in search of a ford which some of the rangers had discovered, about a mile and half distant. While we were waiting for the return of our ferryman, I happened to cast my eyes upon a heap of luggage under a bush, and descried the sleek carcass of the polecat, snugly trussed up, and ready for roasting before the evening fire. I could not resist the temptation to plump it into the river, when it sunk to the bottom like a lump of lead; and thus our lodge was relieved from the bad odor which this savory viand had threatened to bring upon it.

Our men having recrossed with their cockle-shell bark, it was drawn on shore, half filled with saddles, saddlebags, and other luggage, amounting to a hundred weight; and being again placed in the water, I was invited to take my seat. It appeared to me pretty much like the embarkation of the wise men of Gotham, who went to sea in a bowl: I stepped in, however, without hesitation, though as cautiously as possible, and sat down on the top of the luggage, the margin of the hide sinking to within a hand-breadth of the water's edge. Rifles, fowling-pieces, and other articles of small bulk, were then handed in, until I protested against receiving any more freight. We then launched forth upon the stream, the bark being towed as before.

It was with a sensation half serious, half comic, that I found myself thus afloat, on the skin of a buffalo, in the midst of a wild river, surrounded by wilderness, and towed along by a half savage, whooping and yelling like a devil incarnate. To please the vanity of little Tonish, I discharged the double-barreled gun, to the right and left, when in the center of the stream. The report echoed along the woody shores, and was answered by shouts from some of the rangers, to the great exultation of the little Frenchman, who took to himself the whole glory of this Indian mode of navigation.

Our voyage was accomplished happily; the commissioner was ferried across with equal success, and all our effects were brought over in the same manner. Nothing could equal the vainglorious vaporing of little Tonish, as he strutted about the shore, and exulted in his superior skill and knowledge to the rangers. Beatte, however, kept his proud, saturnine look, without a smile. He had a vast contempt for the ignorance of the rangers, and felt that he had been undervalued by them. His only observation was, "Dey now see de Indian good for someting, anyhow!"

The broad, sandy shore where we had landed was intersected by innumerable tracks of elk, deer, bears, raccoons, turkeys, and water fowl. The river scenery at this place was beautifully diversified, presenting long, shining reaches, bordered by willows and cottonwood trees; rich bottoms, with lofty forests; among which towered enormous plane trees, and the distance was closed in by high embowered promontories. The foliage had a yellow autumnal tint, which gave to the sunny landscape the golden tone of one of the landscapes of Claude Lorraine. There was animation given to the scene by a raft of logs and branches, on which the captain and his prime companion, the doctor, were ferrying their effects across the stream; and by a long line of rangers on horseback, fording the river obliquely, along a series of sandbars, about a mile and a half distant.

CHAPTER THIRTEEN

THE CAMP OF THE GLEN

CAMP GOSSIP—PAWNEES AND THEIR HABITS—A HUNTER'S
ADVENTURE—HORSES FOUND, AND MEN LOST

BEING joined by the captain and some of the rangers, we struck into the woods for about half a mile, and then entered a wild, rocky dell, bordered by two lofty ridges of limestone, which narrowed as we advanced, until they met and united; making almost an angle. Here a fine spring of water rose among the rocks, and fed a silver rill that ran the whole length of the dell, freshening the grass with which it was carpeted.

In this rocky nook we encamped, among tall trees. The rangers gradually joined us, straggling through the forest singly or in groups; some on horseback, some on foot, driving their horses before them, heavily laden with baggage, some dripping wet, having fallen into the river; for they had experienced much fatigue and trouble from the length of the ford, and the depth and rapidity of the stream. They looked not unlike banditti returning with their plunder, and the wild dell was a retreat worthy to receive them. The effect was heightened after dark, when the light of the fires was cast upon rugged looking groups of men and horses; with baggage tumbled in heaps, rifles piled against the trees, and saddles, bridles, and powder-horns hanging about their trunks.

At the encampment we were joined by the young count and his companion, and the young half-breed, Antoine, who had all passed successfully by the ford. To my annoyance, however, I discovered that both of my horses were missing. I had supposed them in the charge of Antoine; but he, with characteristic carelessness, had paid no heed to them, and they had probably wandered from the line on the opposite side of the river. It was arranged that Beatte and Antoine should recross the river at an early hour of the morning in search of them.

A fat buck and a number of wild turkeys being brought into the camp, we managed, with the addition of a cup of coffee, to make a comfortable supper; after which I repaired to the captain's lodge, which was a kind of council fire and gossiping place for the veterans of the camp.

As we were conversing together, we observed, as on former nights, a dusky, red glow in the west, above the summits of the surrounding cliffs. It was again attributed to Indian fires on the prairies; and supposed to be on the western side of the Arkansas. If so, it was thought they must be made by some party of Pawnees, as the Osage hunters seldom ventured in that quarter. Our half-breeds, however, pronounced them Osage fires; and that they were on the opposite side of the Arkansas.

The conversation now turned upon the Pawnees, into whose hunting grounds we were about entering. There is always some wild untamed tribe of Indians who form, for a time, the terror of a frontier, and about whom all kinds of fearful stories are told. Such, at present, was the case with the Pawnees, who rove the regions between the Arkansas and the Red River, and the prairies of Texas. They were represented as admirable horsemen, and always on horseback; mounted on fleet and hardy steeds, the wild race of the prairies. With these they roam the great plains that extend about the Arkansas, the Red River, and through Texas, to the Rocky Mountains; sometimes engaged in hunting the deer and buffalo, sometimes in warlike and predatory expedi· tions; for, like their counterparts, the sons of Ishmael, their hand is against every one, and every one's hand against them. Some of them have no fixed habitation, but dwell in tents of skin, easily packed up and transported, so that they are here to-day, and away, no one knows where, to-morrow.

One of the veteran hunters gave several anecdotes of their

mode of fighting. Luckless, according to his account, is the band of weary traders or hunters descried by them, in the midst of a prairie. Sometimes they will steal upon them by stratagem, hanging with one leg over the saddle, and their bodies concealed; so that their troop at a distance has the appearance of a gang of wild horses. When they have thus gained sufficiently upon the enemy, they will suddenly raise themselves in their saddles, and come like a rushing blast, all fluttering with feathers, shaking their mantles, brandishing their weapons, and making hideous yells. In this way, they seek to strike a panic into the horses, and put them to the scamper, when they will pursue and carry them off in triumph.

The best mode of defense, according to this veteran woodsman, is to get into the covert of some wood or thicket; or if there be none at hand, to dismount, tie the horses firmly head to head in a circle, so that they cannot break away and scatter, and resort to the shelter of a ravine, or make a hollow in the sand, where they may be screened from the shafts of the Pawnees. The latter chiefly use the bow and arrow, and are dexterous archers; circling round and round their enemy, and lanching their arrows when at full speed. They are chiefly formidable on the prairies, where they have free career for their horses, and no trees to turn aside their arrows. They will rarely follow a flying enemy into the forest.

Several anecdotes, also, were given, of the secrecy and caution with which they will follow, and hang about the camp of an enemy, seeking a favorable moment for plunder or attack.

"We must now begin to keep a sharp lookout," said the captain. "I must issue written orders that no man shall hunt without leave, or fire off a gun, on pain of riding a wooden horse with a sharp back. I have a wild crew of young fellows, unaccustomed to frontier service. It will be difficult to teach them caution. We are now in the land of a silent, watchful, crafty people, who, when we least suspect it, may be around us, spying out all our movements, and ready to pounce upon all stragglers."

"How will you be able to keep your men from firing, if they see game while strolling round the camp?" asked one of the rangers.

"They must not take their guns with them unless they are on duty, or have permission."

"Ah, captain!" cried the ranger, "that will never do for me. Where I go, my rifle goes. I never like to leave it behind; it's like a part of myself. There's no one will take such care of it as I, and there's nothing will take such care of me as my rifle."

"There's truth in all that," said the captain, touched by a true hunter's sympathy. "I've had my rifle pretty nigh as long as I have had my wife, and a faithful friend it has been to me."

Here the doctor, who is as keen a hunter as the captain, joined in the conversation: "A neighbor of mine says, next to my rifle, I'd as leave lend you my wife."

"There's few," observed the captain, "that take care of their rifles as they ought to be taken care of."

"Or of their wives either," replied the doctor, with a wink.

"That's a fact," rejoined the captain.

Word was now brought that a party of four rangers, headed by "Old Ryan," were missing. They had separated from the main body, on the opposite side of the river, when searching for a ford, and had straggled off, nobody knew whither. Many conjectures were made about them, and some apprehensions expressed for their safety.

"I should send to look after them," said the captain, "but old Ryan is with them, and he knows how to take care of himself and of them too. If it were not for him I would not give much for the rest; but he is as much at home in the woods or on a prairie as he would be in his own farmyard. He's never lost, wherever he is. There's a good gang of them to stand by one another; four to watch and one to take care of the fire."

"It's a dismal thing to get lost at night in a strange and wild country," said one of the younger rangers.

"Not if you have one or two in company," said an older one. "For my part, I could feel as cheerful in this hollow as in my own home, if I had but one comrade to take turns to watch and keep the fire going. I could lie here for hours, and gaze up to that blazing star there, that seems to look down into the camp as if it were keeping guard over it."

"Ay, the stars are a kind of company to one, when you have to keep watch alone. That's a cheerful star, too, somehow; that's the evening star, the planet Venus they call it, I think."

"If that's the planet Venus," said one of the council, who, I believe, was the psalm-singing schoolmaster, "it bodes us no good; for I recollect reading in some book that the Pawnees worship that star, and sacrifice their prisoners to it. So I should not feel the better for the sight of that star in this part of the country."

"Well," said the sergeant, a thoroughbred woodsman, "star or no star, I have passed many a night alone in a wilder place than this, and slept sound too, I'll warrant you. Once, however, I had rather an uneasy time of it. I was belated in passing through a tract of wood, near the Tombigbee River; so I struck a light, made a fire, and turned my horse loose, while I stretched myself to sleep. By-and-by, I heard the wolves howl. My horse came crowding near me for protection, for he was terribly frightened. I drove him off, but he returned, and drew nearer and nearer, and stood looking at me and at the fire, and dozing, and nodding, and tottering on his forefeet, for he was powerful tired. After a while, I heard a strange dismal cry. I thought at first it might be an owl. I heard it again, and then I knew it was not an owl, but must be a panther. I felt rather awkward, for I had no weapon but a double-bladed penknife. I, however, prepared for defense in the best way I could, and piled up small brands from the fire, to pepper him with, should he come nigh. The company of my horse now seemed a comfort to me; the poor creature laid down beside me and soon fell asleep, being so tired. I kept watch, and nodded and dozed, and started awake, and looked round, expecting to see the glaring eyes of the panther close upon me; but somehow or other fatigue got the better of me and I fell asleep outright. In the morning I found the tracks of a panther within sixty paces. They were as large as my two fists. He had evidently been walking backward and forward, trying to make up his mind to attack me; but luckily he had not courage."

October 16th.—I awoke before daylight. The moon was shining feebly down into the glen, from among light drifting clouds; the camp fires were nearly burned out, and the men lying about them, wrapped in blankets. With the first streak of day, our huntsman, Beatte, with Antoine, the young half-breed, set off to recross the river, in search of the stray horses, in company with several rangers who had left their rifles on the opposite shore. As the ford was deep, and they were obliged to cross in a diagonal line, against a rapid current, they had to be mounted on the tallest and strongest horses.

By eight o'clock Beatte returned. He had found the horses, but had lost Antoine. The latter, he said, was a boy, a greenhorn, that knew nothing of the woods. He had wandered out of sight of him and got lost. However, there were plenty more for him to fall in company with, as some of the rangers had gone astray also, and old Ryan and his party had not returned.

We waited until the morning was somewhat advanced, in hopes of being rejoined by the stragglers, but they did not make their appearance. The captain observed, that the Indians on the opposite side of the river were all well disposed to the whites; so that no serious apprehensions need be entertained for the safety of the missing. The greatest danger was, that their horses might be stolen in the night by straggling Osages. He determined, therefore, to proceed, leaving a rear-guard in the camp, to await their arrival.

I sat on a rock that overhung the spring at the upper part of the dell, and amused myself by watching the changing scene before me. First, the preparations for departure. Horses driven in from the purlieus of the camp; rangers riding about among rocks and bushes in quest of others that had strayed to a distance; the bustle of packing up camp equipage, and the clamor after kettles and frying-pans borrowed by one mess from another, mixed up with oaths and exclamations at restive horses, or others that had wandered away to graze after being packed, among which the voice of our little Frenchman, Tonish, was particularly to be distinguished.

The bugle sounded the signal to mount and march. The troop filed off in irregular line down the glen, and through the open forest, winding and gradually disappearing among the trees, though the clamor of voices and the notes of the bugle could be heard for some time afterward. The rearguard remained under the trees in the lower part of the dell, some on horseback, with their rifles on their shoulders; others seated by the fire or lying on the ground, gossiping in a low, lazy tone of voice, their horses unsaddled, standing and dozing around, while one of the rangers, profiting by this interval of leisure, was shaving himself before a pocket mirror stuck against the trunk of a tree.

The clamor of voices and the notes of the bugle at length died away, and the glen relapsed into quiet and silence, broken occasionally by the low murmuring tone of the group around the fire, or the pensive whistle of some laggard among the trees; or the rustling of the yellow leaves, which the lightest breath of air brought down in wavering showers, a sign of the departing glories of the year.

CHAPTER FOURTEEN

DEER-SHOOTING—LIFE ON THE PRAIRIES—BEAUTIFUL EN-
CAMPMENT—HUNTER'S LUCK—ANECDOTES OF THE
DELAWARES AND THEIR SUPERSTITIONS

HAVING passed through the skirt of woodland bordering
the river, we ascended the hills, taking a westerly course
through an undulating country of "oak openings," where
the eye stretched over wide tracts of hill and dale, diversified
by forests, groves, and clumps of trees. As we were proceeding at a slow pace, those who were at the head of the
line descried four deer grazing on a grassy slope about half
a mile distant. They apparently had not perceived our approach, and continued to graze in perfect tranquillity. A
young ranger obtained permission from the captain to go in
pursuit of them, and the troop halted in lengthened line,
watching him in silence. Walking his horse slowly and
cautiously, he made a circuit until a screen of wood inter-
vened between him and the deer. Dismounting then, he
left his horse among the trees, and creeping round a knoll,
was hidden from our view. We now kept our eyes intently
fixed on the deer, which continued grazing, unconscious of
their danger. Presently there was the sharp report of a rifle;
a fine buck made a convulsive bound and fell to the earth;
his companion scampered off. Immediately our whole line
of march was broken; there was a helter-skelter galloping
of the youngsters of the troop, eager to get a shot at the
fugitives; and one of the most conspicuous personages in the
chase was our little Frenchman Tonish, on his silver-gray;
having abandoned his pack-horses at the first sight of the
deer. It was some time before our scattered forces could be
recalled by the bugle and our march resumed.

Two or three times in the course of the day we were interrupted by hurry-scurry scenes of the kind. The young men of the troop were full of excitement on entering an unexplored country abounding in game, and they were too little accustomed to discipline or restraint to be kept in order. No one, however, was more unmanageable than Tonish. Having an intense conceit of his skill as a hunter, and an irrepressible passion for display, he was continually sallying forth, like an ill-broken hound, whenever any game was started, and had as often to be whipped back.

At length his curiosity got a salutary check. A fat doe came bounding along in full view of the whole line. Tonish dismounted, leveled his rifle, and had a fair shot. The doe kept on. He sprang upon his horse, stood up on the saddle like a posture master, and continued gazing after the animal as if certain to see it fall. The doe, however, kept on its way rejoicing; a laugh broke out along the line, the little Frenchman slipped quietly into his saddle, began to belabor and blaspheme the wandering pack-horses, as if they had been to blame, and for some time we were relieved from his vaunting and vaporing.

In one place of our march we came to the remains of an old Indian encampment, on the banks of a fine stream, with the moss-grown skulls of deer lying here and there about it. As we were in the Pawnee country, it was supposed, of course, to have been a camp of those formidable rovers; the doctor, however, after considering the shape and disposition of the lodges, pronounced it the camp of some bold Delawares, who had probably made a brief and dashing excursion into these dangerous hunting grounds.

Having proceeded some distance further, we observed a couple of figures on horseback, slowly moving parallel to us along the edge of a naked hill about two miles distant; and apparently reconnoitering us. There was a halt, and much gazing and conjecturing. Were they Indians? If Indians, were they Pawnees? There is something exciting to the imagination and stirring to the feelings, while traversing these hostile plains, in seeing a horseman prowling along the horizon. It is like descrying a sail at sea in time of war, when it may be either a privateer or a pirate. Our conjectures were soon set at rest by reconnoitering the two horsemen through a small spyglass, when they proved to be two of the men we had left at the camp, who had set out to rejoin us, and had wandered from the track.

Our march this day was animating and delightful. We were in a region of adventure; breaking our way through a country hitherto untrodden by white men, excepting perchance by some solitary trapper. The weather was in its perfection, temperate, genial and enlivening; a deep blue sky with a few light feathery clouds, an atmosphere of perfect transparency, an air pure and bland, and a glorious country spreading out far and wide in the golden sunshine of an autumnal day; but all silent, lifeless, without a human habitation, and apparently without a human inhabitant! It was as if a ban hung over this fair but fated region. The very Indians dared not abide here, but made it a mere scene of perilous enterprise, to hunt for a few days, and then away.

After a march of about fifteen miles west we encamped in a beautiful peninsula, made by the windings and doublings of a deep, clear, and almost motionless brook, and covered by an open grove of lofty and magnificent trees. Several hunters immediately started forth in quest of game before the noise of the camp should frighten it from the vicinity. Our man, Beatte, also took his rifle and went forth alone, in a different course from the rest.

For my own part I laid on the grass under the trees, and built castles in the clouds, and indulged in the very luxury of rural repose. Indeed I can scarcely conceive a kind of life more calculated to put both mind and body in a healthful tone. A morning's ride of several hours diversified by hunting incidents; an encampment in the afternoon under some noble grove on the borders of a stream; an evening banquet of venison, fresh killed, roasted, or broiled on the coals; turkeys just from the thickets and wild honey from the trees;

and all relished with an appetite unknown to the gourmets of the cities. And at night—such sweet sleeping in the open air, or waking and gazing at the moon and stars, shining between the trees!

On the present occasion, however, we had not much reason to boast of our larder. But one deer had been killed during the day, and none of that had reached our lodge. We were fain, therefore, to stay our keen appetites by some scraps of turkey brought from the last encampment, eked out with a slice or two of salt pork. This scarcity, however, did not continue long. Before dark a young hunter returned well laden with spoil. He had shot a deer, cut it up in an artist-like style, and, putting the meat in a kind of sack made of the hide, had slung it across his shoulder and trudged with it to camp.

Not long after, Beatte made his appearance with a fat doe across his horse. It was the first game he had brought in, and I was glad to see him with a trophy that might efface the memory of the polecat. He laid the carcass down by our fire without saying a word, and then turned to unsaddle his horse; nor could any questions from us about his hunting draw from him more than laconic replies. If Beatte, however, observed this Indian taciturnity about what he had done, Tonish made up for it by boasting of what he meant to do. Now that we were in a good hunting country he meant to take the field, and, if we would take his word for it, our lodge would henceforth be overwhelmed with game. Luckily this talking did not prevent his working, the doe was skillfully dissected, several fat ribs roasted before the fire, the coffee kettle replenished, and in a little while we were enabled to indemnify ourselves luxuriously for our late meager repast.

The captain did not return until late, and he returned empty handed. He had been in pursuit of his usual game, the deer, when he came upon the tracks of a gang of about sixty elk. Having never killed an animal of the kind, and the elk being at this moment an object of ambition among all the veteran hunters of the camp, he abandoned his pursuit of the deer, and followed the newly discovered track. After some time he came in sight of the elk, and had several fair chances of a shot, but was anxious to bring down a large buck which kept in the advance. Finding at length there was danger of the whole gang escaping him, he fired at a doe. The shot took effect, but the animal had sufficient strength to keep on for a time with its companions. From the tracks of blood he felt confident it was mortally wounded, but evening came on, he could not keep the trail, and had to give up the search until morning.

Old Ryan and his little band had not yet rejoined us, neither had our young half-breed Antoine made his appearance. It was determined, therefore, to remain at our encampment for the following day, to give time for all stragglers to arrive.

The conversation this evening, among the old huntsmen, turned upon the Delaware tribe, one of whose encampments we had passed in the course of the day; and anecdotes were given of their prowess in war and dexterity in hunting. They used to be deadly foes of the Osages, who stood in great awe of their desperate valor, though they were apt to attribute it to a whimsical cause. "Look at the Delawares," would they say, "dey got short leg—no can run—must stand and fight a great heap." In fact the Delawares are rather short legged, while the Osages are remarkable for length of limb.

The expeditions of the Delawares, whether of war or hunting, are wide and fearless; a small band of them will penetrate far into these dangerous and hostile wilds, and will push their encampments even to the Rocky Mountains. This daring temper may be in some measure encouraged by one of the superstitions of their creed. They believe that a guardian spirit, in the form of a great eagle, watches over them, hovering in the sky, far out of sight. Sometimes, when well pleased with them, he wheels down into the lower regions, and may be seen circling with wide spread wings against the white clouds; at such times the seasons are propitious, the corn grows finely, and they have great success in hunting. Sometimes, however, he is angry, and then he vents his rage in the thunder, which is his voice, and the lightning, which is the flashing of his eye, and strikes dead the object of his displeasure.

The Delawares make sacrifices to this spirit, who occasionally lets drop a feather from his wing in token of satisfaction. These feathers render the wearer invisible, and invulnerable. Indeed, the Indians generally consider the feathers of the eagle possessed of occult and sovereign virtues.

At one time a party of the Delawares, in the course of a bold excursion into the Pawnee hunting grounds, were surrounded on one of the great plains and nearly destroyed. The remnant took refuge on the summit of one of those isolated and conical hills which rise almost like artificial mounds, from the midst of the prairies. Here the chief warrior, driven almost to despair, sacrificed his horse to the tutelar spirit. Suddenly an enormous eagle, rushing down from the sky, bore off the victim in his talons, and, mounting into the air, dropped a quill feather from his wing. The chief caught it up with joy, bound it to his forehead, and, leading his followers down the hill, cut his way through the enemy with great slaughter, and without any one of his party receiving a wound.

CHAPTER FIFTEEN

THE SEARCH FOR THE ELK—PAWNEE STORIES

WITH the morning dawn, the prime hunters of the camp were all on the alert, and set off in different directions, to beat up the country for game. The captain's brother, Sergeant Bean, was among the first, and returned before breakfast with success, having killed a fat doe almost within the purlieus of the camp.

When breakfast was over, the captain mounted his horse, to go in quest of the elk which he had wounded on the preceding evening; and which, he was persuaded, had received its death-wound. I determined to join him in the search, and we accordingly sallied forth together, accompanied also by his brother, the sergeant, and a lieutenant. Two rangers followed on foot, to bring home the carcass of the doe which the sergeant had killed. We had not ridden far, when we came to where it lay, on the side of a hill, in the midst of a beautiful woodland scene. The two rangers immediately fell to work, with true hunters' skill, to dismember it, and prepare it for transportation to the camp, while we continued on our course. We passed along sloping hill-sides, among skirts of thicket and scattered forest trees, until we came to a place where the long herbage was pressed down with numerous elk beds. Here the captain had first roused the gang of elks, and, after looking about diligently for a little while, he pointed out their "trail," the footprints of which were as large as those of horned cattle. He now put himself upon the track, and went quietly forward, the rest of us following him in Indian file. At length he halted at the place where the elk had been when shot at. Spots of blood on the surrounding herbage showed that the shot had been effective. The wounded animal had evidently kept for some distance with the rest of the herd, as could be seen by sprinklings of blood here and there, on the shrubs and weeds bordering the trail. These at length suddenly disappeared. "Somewhere hereabout," said the captain, "the elk must have turned off from the gang. Whenever they feel themselves mortally wounded, they will turn aside and seek some out-of-the-way place to die alone."

There was something in this picture of the last moments of a wounded deer to touch the sympathies of one not hardened to the gentle disports of the chase; such sympathies, however, are but transient. Man is naturally an animal of prey; and, however changed by civilization, will readily relapse into his instinct for destruction. I found my ravenous and sanguinary propensities daily growing stronger upon the prairies.

After looking about for a little while, the captain succeeded in finding the separate trail of the wounded elk, which turned off almost at right angles from that of the herd, and entered an open forest of scattered trees. The traces of blood became more faint and rare, and occurred at greater distances; at length they ceased altogether, and the ground was so hard, and the herbage so much parched and withered, that the footprints of the animal could no longer be perceived.

"The elk must lie somewhere in this neighborhood," said the captain, "as you may know by those turkey-buzzards wheeling about in the air: for they always hover in that way above some carcass. However, the dead elk cannot get away, so let us follow the trail of the living ones: they may have halted at no great distance, and we may find them grazing, and get another crack at them."

We accordingly returned, and resumed the trail of the elks, which led us a straggling course over hill and dale, covered with scattered oaks. Every now and then we would catch a glimpse of a deer bounding away across some glade of the forest, but the captain was not to be diverted from his elk hunt by such inferior game. A large flock of wild turkeys, too, were roused by the trampling of our horses; some scampered off as fast as their long legs could carry them; others fluttered up into the trees, where they remained with outstretched necks, gazing at us. The captain would not allow a rifle to be discharged at them, lest it should alarm the elk, which he hoped to find in the vicinity. At length we came to where the forest ended in a steep bank, and the Red Fork wound its way below us, between broad sandy shores. The trail descended the bank, and we could trace it, with our eyes, across the level sands, until it terminated in the river, which, it was evident, the gang had forded on the preceding evening.

"It is needless to follow on any further," said the captain. "The elk must have been much frightened, and, after crossing the river, may have kept on for twenty miles without stopping."

Our little party now divided, the lieutenant and sergeant making a circuit in quest of game, and the captain and myself taking the direction of the camp. On our way, we came to a buffalo track, more than a year old. It was not wider than an ordinary footpath, and worn deep into the soil; for these animals follow each other in single file. Shortly afterward, we met two·rangers on foot, hunting. They had wounded an elk, but he had escaped; and in pursuing him, had found the one shot by the captain on the preceding evening. They turned back and conducted us to it. It was a noble animal, as large as a yearling heifer, and lay in an open part of the forest, about a mile and a half distant from the place where it had been shot. The turkey-buzzards, which we had previously noticed, were wheeling in the air above it. The observation of the captain seemed verified. The poor animal, as life was ebbing away, had apparently abandoned its unhurt companions and turned aside to die alone.

The captain and the two rangers forthwith fell to work, with their hunting-knives, to flay and cut up the carcass. It was already tainted on the inside, but ample collops were cut from the ribs and haunches, and laid in a heap on the outstretched hide. Holes were then cut along the border of the hide, raw thongs were passed through them and the whole drawn up like a sack, which was swung behind the captain's saddle. All this while, the turkey-buzzards were soaring overhead, waiting for our departure to swoop down and banquet on the carcass.

The wreck of the poor elk being thus dismantled, the captain and myself mounted our horses, and jogged back to the camp, while the two rangers resumed their hunting.

On reaching the camp, I found there our young half-breed, Antoine. After separating from Beatte, in the search after the stray horses on the other side of the Arkansas, he had fallen upon a wrong track, which he followed for several miles, when he overtook old Ryan and his party, and found he had been following their traces.

They all forded the Arkansas about eight miles above our crossing place, and found their way to our late encampment in the glen, where the rear-guard we had left behind was waiting for them. Antoine, being well mounted, and somewhat impatient to rejoin us, had pushed on alone, following our trail, to our present encampment, and bringing the carcass of a young bear which he had killed.

Our camp, during the residue of the day, presented a mingled picture of bustle and repose. Some of the men were busy round the fires, jerking and roasting venison and bear's meat, to be packed up as a future supply. Some were stretching and dressing the skins of the animals they had killed; others were washing their clothes in the brook, and hanging them on the bushes to dry; while many were lying on the grass and lazily gossiping in the shade. Every now and then a hunter would return, on horseback or on foot, laden with game, or empty handed. Those who brought home any spoil deposited it at the captain's fire, and then filed off to their respective messes, to relate their day's exploits to their companions. The game killed at this camp consisted of six deer, one elk, two bears, and six or eight turkeys.

During the last two or three days, since their wild Indian achievement in navigating the river, our retainers had risen in consequence among the rangers; and now I found Tonish making himself a complete oracle among some of the raw and inexperienced recruits, who had never been in the wilderness. He had continually a knot hanging about him, and listening to his extravagant tales about the Pawnees, with whom he pretended to have had fearful encounters. His representations, in fact, were calculated to inspire his hearers with an awful idea of the foe into whose lands they were intruding. According to his accounts, the rifle of the white man was no match for the bow and arrow of the Pawnee. When the rifle was once discharged, it took time and trouble

to load it again, and in the meantime the enemy could keep
on lanching his shafts as fast as he could draw his bow.
Then the Pawnee, according to Tonish, could shoot with un-
erring aim, three hundred yards, and send his arrow clean
through and through a buffalo; nay, he had known a Pawnee
shaft pass through one buffalo and wound another. And
then the way the Pawnees sheltered themselves from the
shots of their enemy: they would hang with one leg over the
saddle, crouching their bodies along the opposite side of their
horse, and would shoot their arrows from under his neck,
while at full speed!

If Tonish was to be believed, there was peril at every step
in these debatable grounds of the Indian tribes. Pawnees
lurked unseen among the thickets and ravines. They had
their scouts and sentinels on the summit of the mounds which
command a view over the prairies, where they lay crouched
in the tall grass; only now and then raising their heads to
watch the movements of any war or hunting party that
might be passing in lengthened line below. At night, they
would lurk round an encampment; crawling through the
grass, and imitating the movements of a wolf, so as to deceive
the sentinel on the outpost, until, having arrived sufficiently
near, they would speed an arrow through his heart, and
retreat undiscovered. In telling his stories, Tonish would
appeal from time to time to Beatte, for the truth of what he
said; the only reply would be a nod or shrug of the shoulders;
the latter being divided in mind between a distaste for the
gasconading spirit of his comrade, and a sovereign contempt
for the inexperience of the young rangers in all that he considered true knowledge.

CHAPTER SIXTEEN

A SICK CAMP—THE MARCH—THE DISABLED HORSE—OLD
RYAN AND THE STRAGGLERS— SYMPTOMS OF CHANGE
OF WEATHER, AND CHANGE OF HUMORS

OCTOBER 18TH.—We prepared to march at the usual hour, but word was brought to the captain that three of the rangers, who had been attacked with the measles, were unable to proceed, and that another one was missing. The last was an old frontiersman, by the name of Sawyer, who had gained years without experience; and having sallied forth to hunt, on the preceding day, had probably lost his way on the prairies. A guard of ten men was, therefore, to take care of the sick, and wait for the straggler. If the former recovered sufficiently in the course of two or three days, they were to rejoin the main body, otherwise to be escorted back to the garrison.

Taking our leave of the sick camp, we shaped our course westward, along the heads of small streams, all wandering, in deep ravines, toward the Red Fork. The land was high and undulating, or "rolling," as it is termed in the West; with a poor hungry soil mingled with the sandstone, which is unusual in this part of the country, and checkered with harsh forests of post-oak and black-jack.

In the course of the morning, I received a lesson on the importance of being chary of one's steed on the prairies. The one I rode on surpassed in action most horses of the troop, and was of great mettle and a generous spirit. In crossing the deep ravines, he would scramble up the steep banks like a cat, and was always for leaping the narrow runs of water. I was not aware of the imprudence of indulging him in such exertions, until, in leaping him across a small brook, I felt him immediately falter beneath me. He limped
* * * 19—VOL. VII.

forward a short distance, but soon fell stark lame, having sprained his shoulder. What was to be done? He could not keep up with the troop, and was too valuable to be abandoned on the prairie. The only alternative was to send him back to join the invalids in the sick camp, and to share their fortunes. Nobody, however, seemed disposed to lead him back, although I offered a liberal reward. Either the stories of Tonish about the Pawnees had spread an apprehension of lurking foes and imminent perils on the prairies; or there was a fear of missing the trail and getting lost. At length two young men stepped forward and agreed to go in company, so that, should they be benighted on the prairies, there might be one to watch while the other slept.

The horse was accordingly consigned to their care, and I looked after him with a rueful eye, as he limped off, for it seemed as if, with him, all strength and buoyancy had departed from me.

I looked round for a steed to supply his place, and fixed my eyes upon the gallant gray which I had transferred at the agency to Tonish. The moment, however, that I hinted about his dismounting and taking up with the supernumerary pony, the little varlet broke out into vociferous remonstrances and lamentations, gasping and almost strangling, in his eagerness to give vent to them. I saw that to unhorse him would be to prostrate his spirit and cut his vanity to the quick. I had not the heart to inflict such a wound, or to bring down the poor devil from his transient vainglory; so I left him in possession of his gallant gray, and contented myself with shifting my saddle to the jaded pony.

I was now sensible of the complete reverse to which a horseman is exposed on the prairies. I felt how completely the spirit of the rider depended upon his steed. I had hitherto been able to make excursions at will from the line, and to gallop in pursuit of any object of interest or curiosity. I was now reduced to the tone of the jaded animal I bestrode, and doomed to plod on patiently and slowly after my file leader. Above all, I was made conscious how unwise it is, on expeditions of the kind, where a man's life may depend upon the strength, and speed, and freshness of his horse, to task the generous animal by any unnecessary exertion of his powers. I have observed that the wary and experienced huntsman and traveler of the prairies is always sparing of his horse, when on a journey; never, except in emergency, putting him off of a walk. The regular journeyings of frontiersmen and Indians, when on a long march, seldom exceed above fifteen miles a day, and are generally about ten or twelve, and they never indulge in capricious galloping. Many of those, however, with whom I was traveling were young and inexperienced, and full of excitement at finding themselves in a country abounding with game. It was impossible to retain them in the sobriety of a march, or to keep them to the line. As we broke our way through the coverts and ravines, and the deer started up and scampered off to the right and left, the rifle balls would whiz after them, and our young hunters dash off in pursuit. At one time they made a grand burst after what they supposed to be a gang of bears, but soon pulled up on discovering them to be black wolves, prowling in company.

After a march of about twelve miles we encamped, a little after midday, on the borders of a brook which loitered through a deep ravine. In the course of the afternoon old Ryan, the Nestor of the camp, made his appearance, followed by his little band of stragglers. He was greeted with joyful acclamations, which showed the estimation in which he was held by his brother woodsmen. The little band came laden with venison; a fine haunch of which the veteran hunter laid, as a present, by the captain's fire.

Our men, Beatte and Tonish, both sallied forth, early in the afternoon, to hunt. Toward evening the former returned with a fine buck across his horse. He laid it down, as usual, in silence, and proceeded to unsaddle and turn his horse loose. Tonish came back without any game, but with much more glory; having made several capital shots, though unluckily the wounded deer had all escaped him.

There was an abundant supply of meat in the camp; for, besides other game, three elk had been killed. The wary and veteran woodsmen were all busy jerking meat against a time of scarcity; the less experienced reveled in present abundance, leaving the morrow to provide for itself.

On the following morning (October 19th), I succeeded in changing my pony and a reasonable sum of money for a strong and active horse. It was a great satisfaction to find myself once more tolerably well mounted. I perceived, however, that there would be little difficulty in making a selection from among the troop, for the rangers had all that propensity for "swapping," or, as they term it, "trading," which pervades the West. In the course of our expedition there was scarcely a horse, rifle, powder-horn, or blanket, that did not change owners several times; and one keen "trader" boasted of having, by dint of frequent bargains, changed a bad horse into a good one, and put a hundred dollars in his pocket.

The morning was lowering and sultry, with low muttering of distant thunder. The change of weather had its effect upon the spirits of the troop. The camp was unusually sober and quiet; there was none of the accustomed farmyard melody of crowing and cackling at daybreak; none of the bursts of merriment, the loud jokes and banterings, that had commonly prevailed during the bustle of equipment. Now and then might be heard a short strain of a song, a faint laugh, or a solitary whistle; but, in general, every one went silently and doggedly about the duties of the camp, or the preparations for departure.

When the time arrived to saddle and mount, five horses were reported as missing; although all the woods and thickets had been beaten up for some distance round the camp. Several rangers were dispatched to "skir" the country round in quest of them. In the meantime, the thunder continued to growl, and we had a passing shower. The horses, like their riders, were affected by the change of weather. They stood here and there about the camp, some saddled and bridled, others loose, but all spiritless and dozing, with stooping head, one hind leg partly drawn up so as to rest on the point of the hoof, and the whole hide reeking with the rain and sending up wreaths of vapor. The men, too, waited in listless groups the return of their comrades who had gone in quest of the horses; now and then turning up an anxious eye to the drifting clouds, which boded an approaching storm. Gloomy weather inspires gloomy thoughts. Some expressed fears that we were dogged by some party of Indians, who had stolen the horses in the night. The most prevalent apprehension, however, was that they had returned on their traces to our last encampment or had started off on a direct line for Fort Gibson. In this respect, the instinct of horses is said to resemble that of the pigeon. They will strike for home by a direct course, passing through tracts of wilderness which they have never before traversed.

After delaying until the morning was somewhat advanced, a lieutenant with a guard was appointed to await the return of the rangers, and we set off on our day's journey, considerably reduced in numbers; much, as I thought, to the discomposure of some of the troop, who intimated that we might prove too weak-handed, in case of an encounter with the Pawnees.

CHAPTER SEVENTEEN

THUNDERSTORM ON THE PRAIRIES—THE STORM ENCAMP-
MENT—NIGHT SCENE—INDIAN STORIES—A
FRIGHTENED HORSE

OUR march for a part of the day lay a little to the south of west, through straggling forests of the kind of low scrubbed trees already mentioned, called "post-oaks" and "black-jacks." The soil of these "oak barrens" is loose and unsound; being little better at times than a mere quicksand, in which, in rainy weather, the horse's hoof slips from side to side, and now and then sinks in a rotten, spongy turf to the fetlock. Such was the case at present in consequence of successive thunder showers, through which we draggled along in dogged silence. Several deer were roused by our approach and scudded across the forest glades; but no one, as formerly, broke the line of march to pursue them. At one time, we passed the bones and horns of a buffalo, and at another time a buffalo track, not above three days old. These signs of the vicinity of this grand game of the prairies had a reviving effect on the spirits of our huntsmen; but it was of transient duration.

In crossing a prairie of moderate extent, rendered little better than a slippery bog by the recent showers, we were overtaken by a violent thunder gust. The rain came rattling upon us in torrents, and spattered up like steam along the ground; the whole landscape was suddenly wrapped in gloom that gave a vivid effect to the intense sheets of lightning, while the thunder seemed to burst over our very heads, and was reverberated by the groves and forests that checkered and skirted the prairie. Man and beast were so pelted, drenched, and confounded, that the line was thrown in complete confusion; some of the horses were so frightened as to be almost unmanageable, and our scattered cavalcade looked like a tempest-tossed fleet, driven hither and thither, at the mercy of wind and wave.

At length, at half-past two o'clock, we came to a halt, and gathering together our forces, encamped in an open and lofty grove, with a prairie on one side and a stream on the other. The forest immediately rang with the sound of the ax, and the crash of falling trees. Huge fires were soon blazing; blankets were stretched before them, by way of tents; booths were hastily reared of bark and skins; every fire had its group drawn close round it, drying and warming themselves, or preparing a comforting meal. Some of the rangers were discharging and cleaning their rifles, which had been exposed to the rain; while the horses, relieved from their saddles and burdens, rolled in the wet grass.

The showers continued from time to time, until late in the evening. Before dark, our horses were gathered in and tethered about the skirts of the camp, within the outposts, through fear of Indian prowlers, who are apt to take advantage of stormy nights for their depredations and assaults. As the night thickened, the huge fires became more and more luminous; lighting up masses of the overhanging foliage, and leaving other parts of the grove in deep gloom. Every fire had its goblin group around it, while the tethered horses were dimly seen, like specters, among the thickets; excepting that here and there a gray one stood out in bright relief.

The grove, thus fitfully lighted up by the ruddy glare of the fires, resembled a vast leafy dome, walled in by opaque darkness; but every now and then two or three quivering flashes of lightning in quick succession would suddenly reveal a vast champaign country, where fields and forests, and running streams, would start, as it were, into existence for a few brief seconds, and, before the eye could ascertain them, vanish again into gloom.

A thunderstorm on a prairie, as upon the ocean, derives grandeur and sublimity from the wild and boundless waste over which it rages and bellows. It is not surprising that these awful phenomena of nature should be objects of superstitious reverence to the poor savages, and that they should consider the thunder the angry voice of the Great Spirit. As our half-breeds sat gossiping round the fire, I drew from them some of the notions entertained on the subject by their Indian friends. The latter declare that extinguished thunderbolts are sometimes picked up by hunters on the prairies, who use them for the heads of arrows and lances, and that any warrior thus armed is invincible. Should a thunderstorm occur, however, during battle, he is liable to be carried away by the thunder, and never heard of more.

A warrior of the Konza tribe, hunting on a prairie, was overtaken by a storm, and struck down senseless by the thunder. On recovering, he beheld the thunderbolt lying on the ground, and a horse standing beside it. Snatching up the bolt, he sprang upon the horse, but found too late that he was astride of the lightning. In an instant he was whisked away over prairies and forests, and streams and deserts, until he was flung senseless at the foot of the Rocky Mountains; whence, on recovering, it took him several months to return to his own people.

This story reminded me of an Indian tradition, related by a traveler, of the fate of a warrior who saw the thunder lying upon the ground, with a beautifully wrought moccasin on each side of it. Thinking he had found a prize, he put on the moccasins; but they bore him away to the land of spirits, whence he never returned.

These are simple and artless tales, but they had a wild and romantic interest heard from the lips of half-savage narrators, round a hunter's fire, on a stormy night, with a forest on one side, and a howling waste on the other; and where, peradventure, savage foes might be lurking in the outer darkness.

Our conversation was interrupted by a loud clap of thunder, followed immediately by the sound of a horse galloping off madly into the waste. Every one listened in mute silence. The hoofs resounded vigorously for a time, but grew fainter and fainter, until they died away in remote distance.

When the sound was no longer to be heard, the listeners turned to conjecture what could have caused this sudden scamper. Some thought the horse had been startled by the thunder; others, that some lurking Indian had galloped off with him. To this it was objected that the usual mode with the Indians is to steal quietly upon the horse, take off his fetters, mount him gently, and walk him off as silently as possible, leading off others, without any unusual stir or noise to disturb the camp.

On the other hand, it was stated as a common practice with the Indians, to creep among a troop of horses when grazing at night, mount one quietly, and then start off suddenly at full speed. Nothing is so contagious among horses as a panic; one sudden break-away of this kind will sometimes alarm the whole troop, and they will set off, helter-skelter, after the leader.

Every one who had a horse grazing on the skirts of the camp was uneasy, lest his should be the fugitive; but it was impossible to ascertain the fact until morning. Those who had tethered their horses felt more secure; though horses thus tied up, and limited to a short range at night, are apt to fall off in flesh and strength, during a long march; and many of the horses of the troop already gave signs of being wayworn.

After a gloomy and unruly night, the morning dawned bright and clear, and a glorious sunrise transformed the whole landscape, as if by magic. The late dreary wilderness brightened into a fine open country, with stately groves, and clumps of oaks of a gigantic size, some of which stood singly, as if planted for ornament and shade, in the midst of rich meadows; while our horses, scattered about, and grazing under them, gave to the whole the air of a noble park. It was difficult to realize the fact that we were so far in the wilds beyond the residence of man. Our encampment, alone, had a savage appearance; with its rude tents of skins and blankets, and its columns of blue smoke rising among the trees.

The first care in the morning was to look after our horses. Some of them had wandered to a distance, but all were fortunately found; even the one whose clattering hoofs had caused such uneasiness in the night. He had come to a halt about a mile from the camp, and was found quietly grazing near a brook. The bugle sounded for departure about half-past eight. As we were in greater risk of Indian molestation the further we advanced, our line was formed with more precision than heretofore. Every one had his station assigned him, and was forbidden to leave it in pursuit of game, without special permission. The pack-horses were placed in the center of the line, and a strong guard in the rear.

CHAPTER EIGHTEEN

A GRAND PRAIRIE—CLIFF CASTLE—BUFFALO TRACKS—
DEER HUNTED BY WOLVES—CROSS TIMBER

AFTER a toilsome march of some distance through a country cut up by ravines and brooks, and entangled by thickets,
we emerged upon a grand prairie. Here one of the characteristic scenes of the Far West broke upon us. An immense extent of grassy, undulating, or, as it is termed, rolling country, with here and there a clump of trees, dimly seen
in the distance like a ship at sea; the landscape deriving sublimity from its vastness and simplicity. To the southwest,
on the summit of a hill, was a singular crest of broken rocks,
resembling a ruined fortress. It reminded me of the ruin of
some Moorish castle, crowning a height in the midst of a
lonely Spanish landscape. To this hill we gave the name
of Cliff Castle.

The prairies of these great hunting regions differed in the
character of their vegetation from those through which I
had hitherto passed. Instead of a profusion of tall flowering
plants and long flaunting grasses, they were covered with
a shorter growth of herbage called buffalo grass, somewhat
coarse, but, at the proper seasons, affording excellent and
abundant pasturage. At present it was growing wiry, and
in many places was too much parched for grazing.

The weather was verging into that serene but somewhat
arid season called the Indian Summer. There was a smoky
haze in the atmosphere that tempered the brightness of the
sunshine into a golden tint, softening the features of the landscape, and giving a vagueness to the outlines of distant objects. This haziness was daily increasing, and was attributed
to the burning of distant prairies by the Indian hunting parties.

We had not gone far upon the prairie before we came to

where deeply worn footpaths were seen traversing the country: sometimes two or three would keep on parallel to each
other, and but a few paces apart. These were pronounced
to be traces of buffaloes, where large droves had passed.
There were tracks also of horses, which were observed with
some attention by our experienced hunters. They could not
be the tracks of wild horses, as there were no prints of the
hoofs of colts; all were full-grown. As the horses evidently
were not shod, it was concluded they must belong to some
hunting party of Pawnees. In the course of the morning, the
tracks of a single horse, with shoes, were discovered. This
might be the horse of a Cherokee hunter, or perhaps a horse
stolen from the whites of the frontier. Thus, in traversing
these perilous wastes, every footprint and dint of hoof be-
comes matter of cautious inspection and' shrewd surmise;
and the question continually is, whether it be the trace of
friend or foe, whether of recent or ancient date, and whether
the being that made it be out of reach, or liable to be encoun ·
tered.

We were getting more and more into the game country:
as we proceeded, we repeatedly saw deer to the right and
left, bounding off for the coverts; but their appearance no
longer excited the same eagerness to pursue. In passing
along a slope of the prairie, between two rolling swells of
land, we came in sight of a genuine natural hunting match.
A pack of seven black wolves and one white one were in full
chase of a buck, which they had nearly tired down. They
crossed the line of our march without apparently perceiving
us; we saw them have a fair run of nearly a mile, gaining
upon the buck until they were leaping upon his haunches,
when he plunged down a ravine. Some of our party gal ·
loped to a rising ground commanding a view of the ravine.
The poor buck was completely beset, some on his flanks,
some at his throat; he made two or three struggles and desperate bounds, but was dragged down, overpowered, and
torn to pieces. The black wolves, in their ravenous hunger
and fury, took no notice of the distant group of horsemen;

but the white wolf, apparently less game, abandoned the prey, and scampered over hill and dale, rousing various deer that were crouched in the hollows, and which bounded off likewise in different directions. It was altogether a wild scene, worthy of the "hunting grounds."

We now came once more in sight of the Red Fork, winding its turbid course between well-wooded hills, and through a vast and magnificent landscape. The prairies bordering on the rivers are always varied in this way with woodland, so beautifully interspersed as to appear to have been laid out by the hand of taste; and they only want here and there a village spire, the battlements of a castle, or the turrets of an old family mansion rising from among the trees, to rival the most ornamented scenery of Europe.

About midday we reached the edge of that scattered belt of forest land, about forty miles in width, which stretches across the country from north to south, from the Arkansas to the Red River, separating the upper from the lower prairies, and commonly called the "Cross Timber." On the skirts of this forest land, just on the edge of a prairie, we found traces of a Pawnee encampment of between one and two hundred lodges, showing that the party must have been numerous. The skull of a buffalo lay near the camp, and the moss which had gathered on it proved that the encampment was at least a year old. About half a mile off we encamped in a beautiful grove, watered by a fine spring and rivulet. Our day's journey had been about fourteen miles.

In the course of the afternoon we were rejoined by two of Lieutenant's King's party, which we had left behind a few days before, to look after stray horses. All the horses had been found, though some had wandered to the distance of several miles. The lieutenant, with seventeen of his companions, had remained at our last night's encampment to hunt, having come upon recent traces of buffalo. They had also seen a fine wild horse, which, however, had galloped off with a speed that defied pursuit.

Confident anticipations were now indulged that on the following day we should meet with buffalo, and perhaps with wild horses, and every one was in spirits. We needed some excitement of the kind, for our young men were growing weary of marching and encamping under restraint, and provisions this day were scanty. The captain and several of the rangers went out hunting, but brought home nothing but a small deer and a few turkeys. Our two men, Beatte and Tonish, likewise went out. The former returned with a deer athwart his horse, which, as usual, he laid down by our lodge, and said nothing. Tonish returned with no game, but with his customary budget of wonderful tales. Both he and the deer had done marvels. Not one had come within the lure of his rifle without being hit in a mortal part, yet, strange to say, every one had kept on his way without flinching. We all determined that, from the accuracy of his aim, Tonish must have shot with charmed balls, but that every deer had a charmed life. The most important intelligence brought by him, however, was that he had seen the fresh tracks of several wild horses. He now considered himself upon the eve of great exploits, for there was nothing upon which he glorified himself more than his skill in horse-catching.

CHAPTER NINETEEN

HUNTER'S ANTICIPATIONS—THE RUGGED FORD—A WILD HORSE

OCTOBER 21ST.—This morning the camp was in a bustle at an early hour: the expectation of falling in with buffalo in the course of the day roused every one's spirit. There was a continual cracking of rifles, that they might be re-loaded: the shot was drawn off from double-barreled guns, and balls were substituted. Tonish, however, prepared chiefly for a campaign against wild horses. He took the field, with a coil of cordage hung at his saddle-bow, and a couple of white wands, something like fishing-rods, eight or ten feet in length, with forked ends. The coil of cordage thus used in hunting the wild horse is called a lariat, and answers to the lasso of South America. It is not flung, however, in the graceful and dexterous Spanish style. The hunter, after a hard chase, when he succeeds in getting almost head and head with the wild horse, hitches the running noose of the lariat over his head by means of the forked stick; then, letting him have the full length of the cord, plays him like a fish, and chokes him into subjection.

All this Tonish promised to exemplify to our full satisfaction; we had not much confidence in his success, and feared he might knock up a good horse in a headlong gallop after a bad one, for, like all the French creoles, he was a merciless hard rider. It was determined, therefore, to keep a sharp eye upon him, and to check his sallying propensities.

We had not proceeded far on our morning's march when we were checked by a deep stream, running along the bottom of a thickly wooded ravine. After coasting it for a couple of miles, we came to a fording place; but to get down to it was the difficulty, for the banks were steep and crumbling, and overgrown with forest trees, mingled with thickets, brambles, and grapevines. At length the leading horseman broke his way through the thicket, and his horse, putting his feet together, slid down the black crumbling bank to the narrow margin of the stream; then floundering across, with mud and water up to the saddle-girths, he scrambled up to the opposite bank, and arrived safe on level ground. The whole line followed pell-mell after the leader, and pushing forward in close order, Indian file, they crowded each other down the bank and into the stream. Some of the horsemen missed the ford, and were soused over head and ears; one was unhorsed, and plumped head foremost into the middle of the stream: for my own part, while pressed forward, and hurried over the bank by those behind me, I was interrupted by a grapevine, as thick as a cable, which hung in a festoon as low as the saddle-bow, and, dragging me from the saddle, threw me among the feet of the trampling horses. Fortunately, I escaped without injury, regained my steed, crossed the stream without further difficulty, and was enabled to join in the merriment occasioned by the ludicrous disasters.

It is at passes like this that occur the most dangerous ambuscades and sanguinary surprises of Indian warfare. A party of savages well placed among the thickets might have made sad havoc among our men, while entangled in the ravine.

We now came out upon a vast and glorious prairie, spreading out beneath the golden beams of an autumnal sun. The deep and frequent traces of buffalo showed it to be one of their favorite grazing grounds; yet none were to be seen. In the course of the morning we were overtaken by the lieutenant and seventeen men, who had remained behind, and who came laden with the spoils of buffaloes; having killed three on the preceding day. One of the rangers, however, had little luck to boast of; his horse having taken fright at sight of the buffaloes, thrown his rider, and escaped into the woods.

The excitement of our hunters, both young and old, now rose almost to fever height; scarce any of them having ever encountered any of this far-famed game of the prairies. Accordingly, when in the course of the day the cry of buffalo! buffalo! rose from one part of the line, the whole troop were thrown in agitation. We were just then passing through a beautiful part of the prairie, finely diversified by hills and slopes, and woody dells, and high, stately groves. Those who had given the alarm pointed out a large black-looking animal, slowly moving along the side of a rising ground, about two miles off. The ever-ready Tonish jumped up, and stood with his feet on the saddle, and his forked sticks in his hands, like a posture-master or scaramouch at a circus, just ready for a feat of horsemanship. After gazing at the animal for a moment, which he could have seen full as well without rising from his stirrups, he pronounced it a wild horse; and dropping again into his saddle was about to dash off full tilt in pursuit, when, to his inexpressible chagrin, he was called back, and ordered to keep to his post, in rear of the baggage horses.

The captain and two of his officers now set off to reconnoiter the game. It was the intention of the captain, who was an admirable marksman, to endeavor to crease the horse; that is to say, to hit him with a rifle ball in the ridge of the neck. A wound of this kind paralyzes a horse for a moment; he falls to the ground, and may be secured before he recovers. It is a cruel expedient, however, for an ill-directed shot may kill or maim the noble animal.

As the captain and his companions moved off laterally and slowly, in the direction of the horse, we continued our course forward; watching intently, however, the movements of the game. The horse moved quietly over the profile of the rising ground, and disappeared behind it. The captain and his party were likewise soon hidden by an intervening hill.

After a time the horse suddenly made his appearance to our right, just ahead of the line, emerging out of a small valley, on a brisk trot; having evidently taken the alarm. At sight of us he stopped short, gazed at us for an instant with surprise, then, tossing up his head, trotted off in fine style, glancing at us first over one shoulder, then over the other, his ample mane and tail streaming in the wind. Having dashed through a skirt of thicket, that looked like a hedgerow, he paused in the open field beyond, glanced back at us again, with a beautiful bend of the neck, snuffed the air, then, tossing his head again, broke into a gallop and took refuge in a wood.

It was the first time I had ever seen a horse scouring his native wilderness in all the pride and freedom of his nature. How different from the poor, mutilated, harnessed, checked, reined-up victim of luxury, caprice, and avarice, in our cities!

After traveling about fifteen miles we encamped about one o'clock, that our hunters might have time to procure a supply of provisions. Our encampment was in a spacious grove of lofty oaks and walnuts, free from underwood, on the border of a brook. While unloading the pack-horses, our little Frenchman was loud in his complaints at having been prevented from pursuing the wild horse, which he would certainly have taken. In the meantime, I saw our half-breed, Beatte, quietly saddle his best horse, a powerful steed of half-savage race, hang a lariat at the saddle-bow, take a rifle and forked stick in hand, and, mounting, depart from the camp without saying a word. It was evident he was going off in quest of the wild horse, but was disposed to hunt alone.

CHAPTER TWENTY

THE CAMP OF THE WILD HORSE

HUNTER'S STORIES — HABITS OF THE WILD HORSE — THE
HALF-BREED AND HIS PRIZE — A HORSE CHASE —
A WILD SPIRIT TAMED

WE had encamped in a good neighborhood for game, as the reports of rifles in various directions speedily gave notice. One of our hunters soon returned with the meat of a doe, tied up in the skin, and slung across his shoulders. Another brought a fat buck across his horse. Two other deer were brought in, and a number of turkeys. All the game was thrown down in front of the captain's fire, to be portioned out among the various messes. The spits and camp kettles were soon in full employ, and throughout the evening there was a scene of hunter's feasting and profusion.

We had been disappointed this day in our hopes of meeting with buffalo, but the sight of the wild horse had been a great novelty, and gave a turn to the conversation of the camp for the evening. There were several anecdotes told of a famous gray horse, which has ranged the prairies of this neighborhood for six or seven years, setting at naught every attempt of the hunters to capture him. They say he can pace and rack (or amble) faster than the fleetest horses can run. Equally marvelous accounts were given of a black horse on the Brazos, who grazed the prairies on that river's bank in Texas. For years he outstripped all pursuit. His fame spread far and wide; offers were made for him to the amount of a thousand dollars; the boldest and most hard-riding hunters tried incessantly to make prize of him, but in vain. At length he fell a victim to his gallantry, being decoyed under a tree by a tame mare, and a noose dropped over his head by a boy perched among the branches.

The capture of a wild horse is one of the most favorite achievements of the prairie tribes; and, indeed, it is from this source that the Indian hunters chiefly supply themselves. The wild horses which range those vast grassy plains, extending from the Arkansas to the Spanish settlements, are of various forms and colors, betraying their various descents. Some resemble the common English stock, and are probably descended from horses which have escaped from our border settlements. Others are of a low but strong make, and are supposed to be of the Andalusian breed, brought out by the Spanish discoverers.

Some fanciful speculatists have seen in them descendants of the Arab stock, brought into Spain from Africa, and thence transferred to this country; and have pleased themselves with the idea that their sires may have been of the pure coursers of the desert that once bore Mahomet and his warlike disciples across the sandy plains of Arabia.

The habits of the Arab seem to have come with the steed. The introduction of the horse on the boundless prairies of the Far West changed the whole mode of living of their inhabitants. It gave them that facility of rapid motion, and of sudden and distant change of place, so dear to the roving propensities of man. Instead of lurking in the depths of gloomy forests, and patiently threading the mazes of a tangled wilderness on foot, like his brethren of the North, the Indian of the West is a rover of the plain; he leads a brighter and more sunshiny life; almost always on horseback, on vast flowery prairies and under cloudless skies.

I was lying by the captain's fire, late in the evening, listening to the stories about those coursers of the prairies, and weaving speculations of my own, when there was a clamor of voices and a loud cheering at the other end of the camp; and word was passed that Beatte, the half-breed, had brought in a wild horse.

In an instant every fire was deserted; the whole camp crowded to see the Indian and his prize. It was a colt about two years old, well grown, finely limbed, with bright prominent eyes and a spirited yet gentle demeanor. He gazed about him with an air of mingled stupefaction and surprise, at the men, the horses, and the camp-fires; while the Indian stood before him with folded arms, having hold of the other end of the cord which noosed his captive, and gazing on him with a most imperturbable aspect. Beatte, as I have before observed, has a greenish olive complexion, with a strongly marked countenance, not unlike the bronze casts of Napoleon; and as he stood before his captive horse with folded arms and fixed aspect he looked more like a statue than a man.

If the horse, however, manifested the least restiveness, Beatte would immediately worry him with the lariat, jerking him first on one side, then on the other, so as almost to throw him on the ground; when he had thus rendered him passive, he would resume his statue-like attitude and gaze at him in silence.

The whole scene was singularly wild; the tall grove, partially illumined by the flashing fires of the camp, the horses tethered here and there among the trees, the carcasses of deer hanging around, and in the midst of all, the wild huntsman and his wild horse, with an admiring throng of rangers, almost as wild.

In the eagerness of their excitement, several of the young rangers sought to get the horse by purchase or barter, and even offered extravagant terms; but Beatte declined all their

offers. "You give great price now," said he, "to-morrow
you be sorry, and take back, and say d—d Indian!"

The young men importuned him with questions about the
mode in which he took the horse, but his answers were dry
and laconic; he evidently retained some pique at having
been undervalued and sneered at by them; and at the same
time looked down upon them with contempt as greenhorns,
little versed in the noble science of woodcraft.

Afterward, however, when he was seated by our fire, I
readily drew from him an account of his exploit; for, though
taciturn among strangers, and little prone to boast of his ac-
tions, yet his taciturnity, like that of all Indians, had its
times of relaxation.

He informed me that, on leaving the camp, he had returned to the place where we had lost sight of the wild horse.
Soon getting upon its track, he followed it to the banks of
the river. Here, the prints being more distinct in the sand,
he perceived that one of the hoofs was broken and defective,
so he gave up the pursuit.

As he was returning to the camp, he came upon a gang
of six horses, which immediately made for the river. He
pursued them across the stream, left his rifle on the river
bank, and putting his horse to full speed, soon came up with
the fugitives. He attempted to noose one of them, but the
lariat hitched on one of his ears, and he shook it off. The
horses dashed up a hill, he followed hard at their heels,
when, of a sudden, he saw their tails whisking in the air,
and they plunged down a precipice. It was too late to stop.
He shut his eyes, held in his breath, and went over with
them—neck or nothing. The descent was between twenty
and thirty feet, but they all came down safe upon a sandy
bottom.

He now succeeded in throwing his noose round a fine
young horse. As he galloped alongside of him, the two horses
passed each side of a sapling, and the end of the lariat was
jerked out of his hand. He regained it, but an intervening
tree obliged him again to let it go. Having once more caught

it, and coming to a more open country, he was enabled to play the young horse with the line until he gradually checked and subdued him, so as to lead him to the place where he had left his rifle.

He had another formidable difficulty in getting him across the river, where both horses stuck for a time in the mire, and Beatte was nearly unseated from his saddle by the force of the current and the struggles of his captive. After much toil and trouble, however, he got across the stream, and brought his prize safe into camp.

For the remainder of the evening the camp remained in a high state of excitement; nothing was talked of but the capture of wild horses; every youngster of the troop was for this harum-scarum kind of chase; every one promised himself to return from the campaign in triumph, bestriding one of these wild coursers of the prairies. Beatte had suddenly risen to great importance; he was the prime hunter, the hero of the day. Offers were made him by the best mounted rangers to let him ride their horses in the chase, provided he would give them a share of the spoil. Beatte bore his honors in silence, and closed with none of the offers. Our stammering, chattering, gasconading little Frenchman, however, made up for his taciturnity by vaunting as much upon the subject as if it were he that had caught the horse. Indeed he held forth so learnedly in the matter, and boasted so much of the many horses he had taken, that he began to be considered an oracle; and some of the youngsters were inclined to doubt whether he were not superior even to the taciturn Beatte.

The excitement kept the camp awake later than usual. The hum of voices, interrupted by occasional peals of laughter, was heard from the groups around the various fires, and the night was considerably advanced before all had sunk to sleep.

With the morning dawn the excitement revived, and Beatte and his wild horse were again the gaze and talk of the camp. The captive had been tied all night to a tree among the other horses. He was again led forth by Beatte,

by a long halter or lariat, and, on his manifesting the least
restiveness, was, as before, jerked and worried into passive
submission. He appeared to be gentle and docile by nature,
and had a beautifully mild expression of the eye. In his
strange and forlorn situation, the poor animal seemed to seek
protection and companionship in the very horse which had
aided to capture him.

Seeing him thus gentle and tractable, Beatte, just as we
were about to march, strapped a light pack upon his back,
by way of giving him the first lesson in servitude. The native pride and independence of the animal took fire at this
indignity. He reared, and plunged, and kicked, and tried
in every way to get rid of the degrading burden. The Indian was too potent for him. At every paroxysm he renewed
the discipline of the halter, until the poor animal, driven to
despair, threw himself prostrate on the ground, and lay motionless, as if acknowledging himself vanquished. A stage
hero, representing the despair of a captive prince, could not
have played his part more dramatically. There was absolutely a moral grandeur in it.

The imperturbable Beatte folded his arms, and stood for
·a time, looking down in silence upon his captive; until seeing him perfectly subdued, he nodded his head slowly,
screwed his mouth into a sardonic smile of triumph, and,
with a jerk of the halter, ordered him to rise. He obeyed,
and from that time forward offered no resistance. During
that day he bore his pack patiently, and was led by the
halter; but in two days he followed voluntarily at large
among the supernumerary horses of the troop.

I could not look without compassion upon this fine young
animal, whose whole course of existence had been so suddenly reversed. From being a denizen of these vast past-
ures, ranging at will from plain to plain and mead to mead,
cropping of every herb and flower, and drinking of every
stream, he was suddenly reduced to perpetual and painful
servitude, to pass his life under the harness and the curb,
amid, perhaps, the din and dust and drudgery of cities. The

transition in his lot was such as sometimes takes place in human affairs, and in the fortunes of towering individuals. One day, a prince of the prairies—the next day, a pack-horse!

CHAPTER TWENTY-ONE

THE FORDING OF THE RED FORK—THE DREARY FORESTS OF THE "CROSS TIMBER"—BUFFALO!

WE left the camp of the wild horse about a quarter before eight, and, after steering nearly south for three or four miles, arrived on the banks of the Red Fork, about seventy-five miles, as we supposed, above its mouth. The river was about three hundred yards wide, wandering among sand-bars and shoals. Its shores, and the long sandy banks that stretched out into the stream, were printed, as usual, with the traces of various animals that had come down to cross it or to drink its waters.

Here we came to a halt, and there was much consultation about the possibility of fording the river with safety, as there was an apprehension of quicksands. Beatte, who had been somewhat in the rear, came up while we were debating. He was mounted on his horse of the half-wild breed, and leading his captive by the bridle. He gave the latter in charge to Tonish, and without saying a word, urged his horse into the stream and crossed it in safety. Everything was done by this man in a similar way, promptly, resolutely, and silently, without a previous promise or an after vaunt.

The troop now followed the lead of Beatte, and reached the opposite shore without any mishap, though one of the pack-horses, wandering a little from the track, came near being swallowed up in a quicksand, and was with difficulty dragged to land.

After crossing the river, we had to force our way, for nearly a mile, through a thick cane-brake, which, at first sight, appeared an impervious mass of reeds and brambles. It was a hard struggle; our horses were often to the saddle-girths in mire and water, and both horse and horseman harassed and torn by bush and brier. Falling, however, upon a buffalo track, we at length extricated ourselves from this morass, and ascended a ridge of land, where we beheld a beautiful open country before us; while to our right, the belt of forest land, called "The Cross Timber," continued stretching away to the southward, as far as the eye could reach. We soon abandoned the open country, and struck into the forest land. It was the intention of the captain to keep on southwest by south, and traverse the Cross Timber diagonally, so as to come out upon the edge of the great western prairie. By thus maintaining something of a southerly direction, he trusted, while he crossed the belt of the forest, he would at the same time approach the Red River.

The plan of the captain was judicious; but he erred from not being informed of the nature of the country. Had he kept directly west, a couple of days would have carried us through the forest land, and we might then have had an easy course along the skirts of the upper prairies, to Red River; by going diagonally, we were kept for many weary days toiling through a dismal series of rugged forests.

The Cross Timber is about forty miles in breadth, and stretches over a rough country of rolling hills, covered with scattered tracts of post-oak and black-jack; with some intervening valleys, which, at proper seasons, would afford good pasturage. It is very much cut up by deep ravines, which, in the rainy seasons, are the beds of temporary streams, tributary to the main rivers, and these are called "branches." The whole tract may present a pleasant aspect in the fresh time of the year, when the ground is covered with herbage; when the trees are in their green leaf, and the glens are enlivened by running streams. Unfortunately, we entered it too late in the season. The herbage was parched; the foliage of the scrubby forests was withered; the whole woodland prospect, as far as the eye could reach, had a brown and arid hue. The fires made on the prairies by the Indian hunters had frequently penetrated these forests, sweeping in light transient flames along the dry grass, scorching and calcining the lower twigs and branches of the trees, and leaving them black and hard, so as to tear the flesh of man and horse that had to scramble through them. I shall not easily forget the mortal toil, and the vexations of flesh and spirit, that we underwent occasionally, in our wanderings through the Cross Timber. It was like struggling through forests of cast iron.

After a tedious ride of several miles, we came out upon an open tract of hill and dale, interspersed with woodland. Here we were roused by the cry of buffalo! buffalo! The effect was something like that of the cry of a sail! a sail! at sea. It was not a false alarm. Three or four of these enormous animals were visible to our sight grazing on the slope of a distant hill.

There was a general movement to set off in pursuit, and it was with some difficulty that the vivacity of the younger men of the troop could be restrained. Leaving orders that the line of march should be preserved, the captain and two of his officers departed at a quiet pace, accompanied by Beatte, and by the ever-forward Tonish; for it was impossible any longer to keep the little Frenchman in check, being half crazy to prove his skill and prowess in hunting the buffalo.

The intervening hills soon hid from us both the game and the huntsmen. We kept on our course in quest of a camping place, which was difficult to be found; almost all the channels of the streams being dry, and the country being destitute of fountain heads.

After proceeding some distance, there was again a cry of buffalo, and two were pointed out on a hill to the left. The captain being absent, it was no longer possible to restrain the ardor of the young hunters. Away several of them dashed, full speed, and soon disappeared among the ravines; the rest kept on, anxious to find a proper place for encampment.

* * * 20—VOL. VII.

Indeed we now began to experience the disadvantages of the season. The pasturage of the prairies was scanty and parched; the pea-vines which grew in the woody bottoms were withered, and most of the "branches" or streams were dried up. While wandering in this perplexity, we were overtaken by the captain and all his party, except Tonish. They had pursued the buffalo for some distance without getting within shot, and had given up the chase, being fearful of fatiguing their horses or being led off too far from camp. The little Frenchman, however, had galloped after them at headlong speed, and the last they saw of him, he was engaged, as it were, yardarm and yardarm, with a great buffalo bull, firing broadsides into him. "I tink dat little man crazy—somehow," observed Beatte, dryly.

CHAPTER TWENTY-TWO

THE ALARM CAMP

WE now came to a halt, and had to content ourselves with an indifferent encampment. It was in a grove of scrub oaks, on the borders of a deep ravine, at the bottom of which were a few scanty pools of water. We were just at the foot of a gradually-sloping hill, covered with half-withered grass, that afforded meager pasturage. In the spot where we had encamped the grass was high and parched. The view around us was circumscribed and much shut in by gently swelling hills.

Just as we were encamping, Tonish arrived, all glorious, from his hunting match; his white horse hung all round with buffalo meat. According to his own account, he had laid low two mighty bulls. As usual, we deducted one-half from his boastings; but, now that he had something real to vaunt about, there was no restraining the valor of his tongue.

After having in some measure appeased his vanity by

boasting of his exploit, he informed us that he had observed the fresh track of horses, which, from various circumstances, he suspected to have been made by some roving band of Pawnees. This caused some little uneasiness. The young men who had left the line of march in pursuit of the two buffaloes had not yet rejoined us; apprehensions were expressed that they might be waylaid and attacked. Our veteran hunter, old Ryan, also, immediately on our halting to encamp, had gone off on foot, in company with a young disciple. "Dat old man will have his brains knocked out by de Pawnees yet," said Beatte. "He tink he know everyting, but he don't know Pawnees, anyhow."

Taking his rifle, the captain repaired on foot to reconnoiter the country from the naked summit of one of the neighboring hills. In the meantime, the horses were hobbled and turned loose to graze; and wood was cut, and fires made, to prepare the evening's repast.

Suddenly there was an alarm of fire in the camp! The flame from one of the kindling fires had caught to the tall dry grass; a breeze was blowing; there was danger that the camp would soon be wrapped in a light blaze. "Look to the horses!" cried one. "Drag away the baggage!" cried another. "Take care of the rifles and powder-horns!" cried a third. All was hurry-scurry and uproar. The horses dashed wildly about; some of the men snatched away rifles and powder-horns, others dragged off saddles and saddle-bags. Meantime, no one thought of quelling the fire, nor indeed knew how to quell it. Beatte, however, and his comrades attacked it in the Indian mode, beating down the edges of the fire with blankets and horse cloths, and endeavoring to prevent its spreading among the grass; the rangers followed their example, and in a little while the flames were happily quelled.

The fires were now properly kindled on places from which the dry grass had been cleared away. The horses were scattered about a small valley, and on the sloping hill-side, cropping the scanty herbage. Tonish was preparing a sumptuous evening's meal from his buffalo meat, promising us a

rich soup and a prime piece of roast beef, but we were
doomed to experience another and more serious alarm.

There was an indistinct cry from some rangers on the
summit of the hill, of which we could only distinguish the
words, "The horses! the horses! get in the horses!"

Immediately a clamor of voices arose; shouts, inquiries,
replies, were all mingled together, so that nothing could be
clearly understood, and every one drew his own inference.

"The captain has started buffaloes," cried one, "and
wants horses for the chase." Immediately a number of
rangers seized their rifles and scampered for the hill-top.
"The prairie is on fire beyond the hill," cried another; "I
see the smoke—the captain means we shall drive the horses
beyond the brook."

By this time a ranger from the hill had reached the skirts
of the camp. He was almost breathless, and could only say
that the captain had seen Indians at a distance.

"Pawnees! Pawnees!" was now the cry among our wild-
headed youngsters. "Drive the horses into camp!" cried
one. "Saddle the horses!" cried another. "Form the line!"
cried a third. There was now a scene of clamor and confusion that baffles all description. The rangers were scampering about the adjacent field in pursuit of their horses. One
might be seen tugging his steed along by a halter; another
without a hat, riding bare-backed; another driving a hobbled
horse before him, that made awkward leaps like a kangaroo.

The alarm increased. Word was brought from the lower
end of the camp that there was a band of Pawnees in a
neighboring valley. They had shot old Ryan through the
head, and were chasing his companion! "No, it was not old
Ryan that was killed—it was one of the hunters that had
been after the two buffaloes." "There are three hundred
Pawnees just beyond the hill," cried one voice. "More,
more!" cried another.

Our situation, shut in among hills, prevented our seeing
to any distance, and left us a prey to all these rumors. A
cruel enemy was supposed to be at hand, and an immediate

attack apprehended. The horses by this time were driven into the camp, and were dashing about among the fires, and trampling upon the baggage. Every one endeavored to prepare for action; but here was the perplexity. During the late alarm of fire the saddles, bridles, rifles, powder-horns, and other equipments, had been snatched out of their places, and thrown helter-skelter among the trees.

"Where is my saddle?" cried one. "Has any one seen my rifle?" cried another. "Who will lend me a ball?" cried a third, who was loading his piece. "I have lost my bullet pouch." "For God's sake help me to girth this horse!" cried another; "he's so restive I can do nothing with him." In his hurry and worry, he had put on the saddle the hind part before!

Some affected to swagger and talk bold; others said nothing, but went on steadily, preparing their horses and weapons, and on these I felt the most reliance. Some were evidently excited and elated with the idea of an encounter with Indians; and none more so than my young Swiss fellow traveler, who had a passion for wild adventure. Our man, Beatte, led his horses in the rear of the camp, placed his rifle against a tree, then seated himself by the fire in perfect silence. On the other hand, little Tonish, who was busy cooking, stopped every moment from his work to play the fanfaron, singing, swearing, and affecting an unusual hilarity, which made me strongly suspect that there was some little fright at bottom, to cause all this effervescence.

About a dozen of the rangers, as soon as they could saddle their horses, dashed off in the direction in which the Pawnees were said to have attacked the hunters. It was now determined, in case our camp should be assailed, to put our horses in the ravine in the rear, where they would be out of danger from arrow or rifle-ball, and to take our stand within the edge of the ravine. This would serve as a trench, and the trees and thickets with which it was bordered would be sufficient to turn aside any shaft of the enemy. The Pawnees, besides, are wary of attacking any covert of the kind; their warfare, as I have already observed, lies in the open prairie, where, mounted upon their fleet horses, they can swoop like hawks upon their enemy, or wheel about him and discharge their arrows. Still I could not but perceive, that, in case of being attacked by such a number of these well-mounted and warlike savages as were said to be at hand, we should be exposed to considerable risk from the inexperience and want of discipline of our newly raised rangers, and from the very courage of many of the younger ones who seemed bent on adventure and exploit.

By this time the captain reached the camp, and every one crowded round him for information. He informed us that he had proceeded some distance on his reconnoitering expedition, and was slowly returning toward the camp, along the brow of a naked hill, when he saw something on the edge of a parallel hill that looked like a man. He paused and watched it; but it remained so perfectly motionless that he supposed it a bush or the top of some tree beyond the hill. He resumed his course, when it likewise began to move in a parallel direction. Another form now rose beside it, of some one who had either been lying down or had just ascended the other side of the hill. The captain stopped and regarded them; they likewise stopped. He then lay down upon the grass, and they began to walk. On his rising, they again stopped, as if watching him. Knowing that the Indians are apt to have their spies and sentinels thus posted on the summit of naked hills, commanding extensive prospects, his doubts were increased by the suspicious movements of these men. He now put his foraging cap on the end of his rifle and waved it in the air. They took no notice of the signal. He then walked on, until he entered the edge of a wood which concealed him from their view. Stopping out of sight for a moment, he again looked forth, when he saw the two men passing swiftly forward. As the hill on which they were walking made a curve toward that on which he stood, it seemed as if they were endeavoring to head him before he should reach the camp. Doubting whether they might not belong to some large party of Indians, either in ambush or moving along the valley beyond the hill, the captain hastened his steps homeward, and, descrying some rangers on an eminence between him and the camp, he called out to them to pass the word to have the horses driven in, as these are generally the first objects of Indian depredation.

Such was the origin of the alarm which had thrown the camp in commotion. Some of those who heard the captain's narration, had no doubt that the men on the hill were Pawnee scouts, belonging to the band that had waylaid the hunters. Distant shots were heard at intervals, which were supposed to be fired by those who had sallied out to rescue their comrades. Several more rangers, having completed their equipments, now rode forth in the direction of the firing; others looked anxious and uneasy.

"If they are as numerous as they are said to be," said one, "and as well mounted as they generally are, we shall be a bad match for them with our jaded horses."

"Well," replied the captain, "we have a strong encampment, and can stand a siege."

"Ay, but they may set fire to the prairie in the night and burn us out of our encampment."

"We will then set up a counter fire!"

The word was now passed that a man on horseback approached the camp.

"It is one of the hunters! It is Clements! He brings buffalo meat!" was announced by several voices as the horseman drew near.

It was, in fact, one of the rangers who had set off in the morning in pursuit of the two buffaloes. He rode into the camp, with the spoils of the chase hanging round his horse, and followed by his companions, all sound and unharmed, and equally well laden. They proceeded to give an account of a grand gallop they had had after the two buffaloes, and how many shots it had cost them to bring one to the ground.

"Well, but the Pawnees—the Pawnees—where are the Pawnees?"

"What Pawnees?"

"The Pawnees that attacked you."

"No one attacked us."

"But have you seen no Indians on your way?"

"Oh, yes, two of us got to the top of a hill to look out for the camp, and saw a fellow on an opposite hill cutting queer antics, who seemed to be an Indian."

"Pshaw! that was I!" said the captain.

Here the bubble burst. The whole alarm had risen from this mutual mistake of the captain and the two rangers. As to the report of the three hundred Pawnees and their attack on the hunters, it proved to be a wanton fabrication, of which no further notice was taken; though the author deserved to have been sought out and severely punished.

There being no longer any prospect of fighting, every one now thought of eating; and here the stomachs throughout the camp were in unison. Tonish served up to us his promised regale of buffalo soup and buffalo beef. The soup was peppered most horribly, and the roast beef proved the bull to have been one of the patriarchs of the prairies; never did I have to deal with a tougher morsel. However, it was our first repast on buffalo meat, so we ate it with a lively faith; nor would our little Frenchman allow us any rest, until he had extorted from us an acknowledgment of the excellence of his cookery; though the pepper gave us the lie in our throats.

The night closed in without the return of old Ryan and his companion. We had become accustomed, however, to the aberrations of this old cock of the woods, and no further solicitude was expressed on his account.

After the fatigues and agitations of the day, the camp soon sunk into a profound sleep, excepting those on guard, who were more than usually on the alert; for the traces recently seen of Pawnees, and the certainty that we were in the midst of their hunting grounds, excited to constant vigilance. About half past ten o'clock we were all startled from sleep by a new alarm. A sentinel had fired off his rifle and run into camp, crying that there were Indians at hand.

Every one was on his legs in an instant. Some seized their rifles; some were about to saddle their horses; some hastened to the captain's lodge, but were ordered back to their respective fires. The sentinel was examined. He declared he had seen an Indian approach, crawling along the ground; whereupon he had fired upon him, and run into camp. The captain gave it as his opinion that the supposed Indian was a wolf; he reprimanded the sentinel for deserting his post, and obliged him to return to it. Many seemed inclined to give credit to the story of the sentinel; for the events of the day had predisposed them to apprehend lurking foes and sudden assaults during the darkness of the night. For a long time they sat round their fires, with rifle in hand, carrying on low, murmuring conversations, and listening for some new alarm. Nothing further, however, occurred; the voices gradually died away; the gossipers nodded and dozed, and sunk to rest; and, by degrees, silence and sleep once more stole over the camp.

CHAPTER TWENTY-THREE

BEAVER DAM—BUFFALO AND HORSE TRACKS—A PAWNEE TRAIL—WILD HORSES—THE YOUNG HUNTER AND THE BEAR—CHANGE OF ROUTE

ON mustering our forces in the morning (October 23d), old Ryan and his comrade were still missing; but the captain had such perfect reliance on the skill and resources of the veteran woodman, that he did not think it necessary to take any measures with respect to him.

Our march this day lay through the same kind of rough rolling country; checkered by brown dreary forests of post-oak, and cut up by deep dry ravines. The distant fires were evidently increasing on the prairies. The wind had been at northwest for several days; and the atmosphere had become so smoky, as in the height of Indian summer, that it was difficult to distinguish objects at any distance.

In the course of the morning we crossed a deep stream with a complete beaver dam, above three feet high, making a large pond, and doubtless containing several families of that industrious animal, though not one showed his nose above water. The captain would not permit this amphibious commonwealth to be disturbed.

We were now continually coming upon the tracks of buffaloes and wild horses; those of the former tended invariably to the south, as we could perceive by the direction of the trampled grass. It was evident we were on the great highway of these migratory herds, but that they had chiefly passed to the southward.

Beatte, who generally kept a parallel course several hundred yards distant from our line of march, to be on the lookout for game, and who regarded every track with the knowing eye of an Indian, reported that he had come upon a very suspicious trail. There were the tracks of men who wore Pawnee moccasins. He had scented the smoke of mingled sumach and tobacco, such as the Indians use. He had observed tracks of horses, mingled with those of a dog; and a mark in the dust where a cord had been trailed along; probably the long bridle, one end of which the Indian horsemen suffer to trail on the ground. It was evident, they were not the tracks of wild horses. My anxiety began to revive about the safety of our veteran hunter Ryan, for I had taken a great fancy to this real old Leatherstocking; every one expressed a confidence, however, that wherever Ryan was, he was safe, and knew how to take care of himself.

We had accomplished the greater part of a weary day's march, and were passing through a glade of the oak openings, when we came in sight of six wild horses, among which I especially noticed two very handsome ones, a gray and a roan. They pranced about, with heads erect, and long flaunting tails, offering a proud contrast to our poor, spiritless, travel-tired steeds. Having reconnoitered us for a moment, they set off at a gallop, passed through a woody dingle, and in a little while emerged once more to view, trotting up a slope about a mile distant.

The sight of these horses was again a sore trial to the vaporing Tonish, who had his lariat and forked stick ready, and was on the point of launching forth in pursuit, on his jaded horse, when he was again ordered back to the pack-horses.

After a day's journey of fourteen miles in a southwest direction, we encamped on the banks of a small clear stream, on the northern border of the Cross Timbers; and on the edge of those vast prairies that extend away to the foot of the Rocky Mountains. In turning loose the horses to graze, their bells were stuffed with grass to prevent their tinkling, lest it might be heard by some wandering horde of Pawnees.

Our hunters now went out in different directions, but without much success, as but one deer was brought into the camp. A young ranger had a long story to tell of his adventures. In skirting the thickets of a deep ravine he had wounded a buck, which he plainly heard to fall among the bushes. He stopped to fix the lock of his rifle, which was out of order, and to reload it; then advancing to the edge of the thicket, in quest of his game, he heard a low growling. Putting the branches aside, and stealing silently forward, he looked down into the ravine and beheld a huge bear dragging the carcass of the deer along the dry channel of a brook, and growling and snarling at four or five officious wolves, who seemed to have dropped in to take supper with him.

The ranger fired at the bear, but missed him. Bruin maintained his ground and his prize, and seemed disposed to make battle. The wolves, too, who were evidently sharp set, drew off to but a small distance. As night was coming on, the young hunter felt dismayed at the wildness and darkness of the place, and the strange company he had fallen in

with; so he quietly withdrew, and returned empty handed
to the camp, where, having told his story, he was heartily
bantered by his more experienced comrades.

In the course of the evening, old Ryan came straggling
into the camp, followed by his disciple, and as usual was
received with hearty gratulations. He had lost himself
yesterday, when hunting, and camped out all night, but had
found our trail in the morning, and followed it up. He had
passed some time at the beaver dam, admiring the skill and
solidity with which it had been constructed. "These bea-
vers," said he, "are industrious little fellows. They are the
knowingest varment as I know; and I'll warrant the pond
was stocked with them."

"Aye," said the captain, "I have no doubt most of the
small rivers we have passed are full of beaver. I would like
to come and trap on these waters all winter."

"But would you not run the chance of being attacked by
Indians?" asked one of the company.

"Oh, as to that, it would be safe enough here, in the
winter time. There would be no Indians here until spring.
I should want no more than two companions. Three persons
are safer than a large number for trapping beaver. They
can keep quiet, and need seldom fire a gun. A bear would
serve them for food for two months, taking care to turn
every part of it to advantage."

A consultation was now held as to our future progress.
We had thus far pursued a western course; and, having
traversed the Cross Timber, were on the skirts of the Great
Western Prairie. We were still, however, in a very rough
country, where food was scarce. The season was so far
advanced that the grass was withered, and the prairies
yielded no pasturage. The pea-vines of the bottoms, also,
which had sustained our horses for some part of the journey,
were nearly gone, and for several days past the poor animals
had fallen off wofully both in flesh and spirit. The Indian
fires on the prairies were approaching us from north, and
south, and west; they might spread also from the east, and

leave a scorched desert between us and the frontier, in which our horses might be famished.

It was determined, therefore, to advance no further to the westward, but to shape our course more to the east, so as to strike the north fork of the Canadian as soon as possible, where we hoped to find abundance of young cane, which, at this season of the year, affords the most nutritious pasturage for the horses; and, at the same time, attracts immense quantities of game. Here then we fixed the limits of our tour to the Far West, being within little more than a day's march of the boundary line of Texas.

CHAPTER TWENTY-FOUR

SCARCITY OF BREAD—RENCONTRE WITH BUFFALOES—WILD TURKEYS—FALL OF A BUFFALO BULL

THE morning broke bright and clear, but the camp had nothing of its usual gayety. The concert of the farmyard was at an end; not a cock crowed, nor dog barked; nor was there either singing or laughing; every one pursued his avocations quietly and gravely. The novelty of the expedition was wearing off. Some of the young men were getting as way-worn as their horses; and most of them, unaccustomed to the hunter's life, began to repine at its privations. What they most felt was the want of bread, their rations of flour having been exhausted for several days. The old hunters, who had often experienced this want, made light of it; and Beatte, accustomed when among the Indians to live for months without it, considered it a mere article of luxury. "Bread," he would say scornfully, "is only fit for a child."

About a quarter before eight o'clock, we turned our backs upon the Far West, and set off in a southeast course along a gentle valley. After riding a few miles, Beatte, who kept parallel with us, along the ridge of a naked hill to our right, called out and made signals, as if something were coming round the hill to intercept us. Some who were near me cried out that it was a party of Pawnees. A skirt of thickets hid the approach of the supposed enemy from our view. We heard a trampling among the brushwood. My horse looked toward the place, snorted and pricked up his ears, when presently a couple of large buffalo bulls, who had been alarmed by Beatte, came crashing through the brake, and making directly toward us. At sight of us they wheeled round and scuttled along a narrow defile of the hill. In an instant half a score of rifles cracked off; there was a universal whoop and halloo, and away went half the troop, helter-skelter in pursuit, and myself among the number. The most of us soon pulled up, and gave over a chase which led through birch and brier and break-neck ravines. Some few of the rangers persisted for a time; but eventually joined the line, slowly lagging one after another. One of them returned on foot; he had been thrown while in full chase; his rifle had been broken in the fall, and his horse, retaining the spirit of the rider, had kept on after the buffalo. It was a melancholy predicament to be reduced to; without horse or weapon in the midst of the Pawnee hunting grounds.

For my own part, I had been fortunate enough recently, by a further exchange, to get possession of the best horse in the troop; a full-blooded sorrel of excellent bottom, beautiful form, and most generous qualities.

In such a situation it almost seems as if a man changes his nature with his horse. I felt quite like another being, now that I had an animal under me, spirited yet gentle, docile to a remarkable degree, and easy, elastic, and rapid in all his movements. In a few days he became almost as much attached to me as a dog; would follow me when I dismounted, would come to me in the morning to be noticed and caressed; and would put his muzzle between me and my book, as I sat reading at the foot of a tree. The feeling I had for this my dumb companion of the prairies, gave me some faint idea of that attachment the Arab is said to entertain for the horse that has borne him about the deserts.

After riding a few miles further, we came to a fine meadow with a broad clear stream winding through it, on the banks of which there was excellent pasturage. Here we at once came to a halt, in a beautiful grove of elms, on the site of an old Osage encampment. Scarcely had we dismounted when a universal firing of rifles took place upon a large flock of turkeys scattered about the grove, which proved to be a favorite roosting-place for these simple birds. They flew to the trees, and sat perched upon their branches, stretching out their long necks, and gazing in stupid astonishment, until eighteen of them were shot down.

In the height of the carnage word was brought that there were four buffaloes in a neighboring meadow. The turkeys were now abandoned for nobler game. The tired horses were again mounted and urged to the chase. In a little while we came in sight of the buffaloes, looking like brown hillocks among the long green herbage. Beatte endeavored to get ahead of them and turn them toward us, that the inexperienced hunters might have a chance. They ran round the base of a rocky hill that hid us from the sight. Some of us endeavored to cut across the hill, but became entrapped in a thick wood, matted with grapevines. My horse, who, under his former rider, had hunted the buffalo, seemed as much excited as myself, and endeavored to force his way through the bushes. At length we extricated ourselves, and galloping over the hill, I found our little Frenchman, Tonish, curveting on horseback round a great buffalo which he had wounded too severely to fly, and which he was keeping employed until we should come up. There was a mixture of the grand and the comic, in beholding this tremendous animal and his fantastic assailant. The buffalo stood with his shaggy front always presented to his foe; his mouth open, his tongue parched, his eyes like coals of fire, and his tail erect with rage; every now and then he would make a faint rush upon his foe, who easily evaded his attack, capering and cutting all kinds of antics before him.

We now made repeated shots at the buffalo, but they

glanced into his mountain of flesh without proving mortal. He made a slow and grand retreat into the shallow river, turning upon his assailants whenever they pressed upon him; and when in the water, took his stand there as if prepared to sustain a siege. A rifle ball, however, more fatally lodged, sent a tremor through his frame. He turned and attempted to wade across the stream, but after tottering a few paces slowly fell upon his side and expired. It was the fall of a hero, and we felt somewhat ashamed of the butchery that had effected it; but, after the first shot or two, we had reconciled it to our feelings, by the old plea of putting the poor animal out of his misery.

Two other buffaloes were killed this evening, but they were all bulls, the flesh of which is meager and hard at this season of the year. A fat buck yielded us more savory meat for our evening's repast.

CHAPTER TWENTY-FIVE

RINGING THE WILD HORSE

WE left the buffalo camp about eight o'clock, and had a toilsome and harassing march of two hours, over ridges of hills, covered with a ragged meager forest of scrub-oaks, and broken by deep gullies. Among the oaks I observed many of the most diminutive size; some not above a foot high, yet bearing abundance of small acorns. The whole of the Cross Timber, in fact, abounds with mast. There is a pine-oak which produces an acorn pleasant to the taste and ripening early in the season.

About ten o'clock in the morning, we came to where this line of rugged hills swept down into a valley, through which flowed the north fork of the Red River. A beautiful meadow about half a mile wide, enameled with yellow autumnal flowers, stretched for two or three miles along the foot of the hills, bordered on the opposite side by the river, whose bank was fringed with cottonwood trees, the bright foliage of which refreshed and delighted the eye, after being wearied by the contemplation of monotonous wastes of brown forest.

The meadow was finely diversified by groves and clumps of trees, so happily dispersed that they seemed as if set out by the hand of art. As we cast our eyes over this fresh and delightful valley, we beheld a troop of wild horses, quietly grazing on a green lawn, about a mile distant to our right, while to our left, at nearly the same distance, were several buffaloes; some feeding, others reposing and ruminating among the high rich herbage, under the shade of a clump of cottonwood trees. The whole had the appearance of a broad beautiful tract of pasture land, on the highly ornamented estate of some gentleman farmer, with his cattle grazing about the lawns and meadows.

A council of war was now held, and it was determined to profit by the present favorable opportunity, and try our hand at the grand hunting maneuver, which is called ringing the wild horse. This requires a large party of horsemen, well mounted. They extend themselves in each direction, singly, at certain distances apart, and gradually form a ring of two or three miles in circumference, so as to surround the game. This has to be done with extreme care, for the wild horse is the most readily alarmed inhabitant of the prairie, and can scent a hunter at a great distance, if to windward.

The ring being formed, two or three ride toward the horses, who start off in an opposite direction. Whenever they approach the bounds of the ring, however, a huntsman presents himself and turns them from their course. In this way they are checked and driven back at every point; and kept galloping round and round this magic circle, until, being completely tired down, it is easy for the hunters to ride up beside them and throw the lariat over their heads. The prime horses of most speed, courage, and bottom, however, are apt to break through and escape, so that, in general, it is the second-rate horses that are taken.

Preparations were now made for a hunt of the kind. The pack-horses were taken into the woods and firmly tied to trees, lest, in a rush of the wild horses, they should break away with them. Twenty-five men were then sent, under the command of a lieutenant, to steal along the edge of the valley within the strip of wood that skirted the hills. They were to station themselves about fifty yards apart, within the edge of the woods, and not advance or show themselves until the horses dashed in that direction. Twenty-five men were sent across the valley, to steal in like manner along the river bank that bordered the opposite side, and to station themselves among the trees. A third party, of about the same number, was to form a line, stretching across the lower part of the valley, so as to connect the two wings. Beatte and our other half-breed, Antoine, together with the ever-officious Tonish, were to make a circuit through the woods so as to get to the upper part of the valley, in the rear of the horses, and to drive them forward into the kind of sack that we had formed, while the two wings should join behind them and make a complete circle.

The flanking parties were quietly extending themselves, out of sight, on each side of the valley, and the residue were stretching themselves, like the links of a chain, across it, when the wild horses gave signs that they scented an enemy; snuffing the air, snorting, and looking about. At length they pranced off slowly toward the river, and disappeared behind a green bank. Here, had the regulations of the chase been observed, they would have been quietly checked and turned back by the advance of a hunter from among the trees; unluckily, however, we had our wild-fire Jack-o'-lantern little Frenchman to deal with. Instead of keeping quietly up the right side of the valley, to get above the horses, the moment he saw them move toward the river, he broke out of the covert of woods, and dashed furiously across the plain in pursuit of them, being mounted on one of the led horses belonging to the count. This put an end to all system. The half-breeds and half a score of rangers joined in the chase.

Away they all went over the green bank; in a moment or two the wild horses reappeared, and came thundering down the valley, with Frenchman, half-breeds, and rangers galloping and yelling like devils behind them. It was in vain that the line drawn across the valley attempted to check and turn back the fugitives. They were too hotly pressed by their pursuers; in their panic they dashed through the line, and clattered down the plain. The whole troop joined in the headlong chase, some of the rangers without hats or caps, their hair flying about their ears, others with handkerchiefs tied round their heads. The buffaloes, who had been calmly ruminating among the herbage, heaved up their huge forms, gazed for a moment with astonishment at the tempest that came scouring down the meadow, then turned and took to heavy-rolling flight. They were soon overtaken; the promiscuous throng were pressed together by the contracting sides of the valley, and away they went, pell-mell, hurry-scurry, wild buffalo, wild horse, wild huntsman, with clang and clatter, and whoop and halloo, that made the forests ring.

At length the buffaloes turned into a green brake on the river bank, while the horses dashed up a narrow defile of the hills, with their pursuers close at their heels. Beatte passed several of them, having fixed his eye upon a fine Pawnee horse, that had his ears slit and saddle-marks upon his back. He pressed him gallantly, but lost him in the woods. Among the wild horses was a fine black mare, far gone with foal. In scrambling up the defile, she tripped and fell. A young ranger sprang from his horse and seized her by the mane and muzzle. Another ranger dismounted, and came to his assistance. The mare struggled fiercely, kicking and biting, and striking with her forefeet, but a noose was slipped over her head, and her struggles were in vain. It was some time, however, before she gave over rearing and plunging and lashing out with her feet on every side. The two rangers then led her along the valley by two long lariats, which enabled them to keep at a sufficient distance on each side to be out of the reach of her hoofs, and whenever she struck out in one direction she was jerked in the other. In this way her spirit was gradually subdued.

As to little Scaramouch Tonish, who had marred the whole scene by his precipitancy, he had been more successful than he deserved, having managed to catch a beautiful cream-colored colt, about seven months old, which had not strength to keep up with its companions. The mercurial little Frenchman was beside himself with exultation. It was amusing to see him with his prize. The colt would rear and kick, and struggle to get free, when Tonish would take him about the neck, wrestle with him, jump on his back, and cut as many antics as a monkey with a kitten. Nothing surprised me more, however, than to witness how soon these poor animals, thus taken from the unbounded freedom of the prairie, yielded to the dominion of man. In the course of two or three days the mare and colt went with the led horses, and became quite docile.

CHAPTER TWENTY-SIX

FORDING OF THE NORTH FORK—DREARY SCENERY OF THE CROSS TIMBER—SCAMPER OF HORSES IN THE NIGHT— OSAGE WAR PARTY—EFFECTS OF A PEACE HARANGUE —BUFFALO—WILD HORSE

RESUMING our march, we forded the North Fork, a rapid stream, and of a purity seldom to be found in the rivers of the prairies. It evidently had its sources in high land, well supplied with springs. After crossing the river, we again ascended among hills, from one of which we had an extensive view over this belt of cross timber, and a cheerless prospect it was; hill beyond hill, forest beyond forest, all of one sad russet hue—excepting that here and there a line of green cottonwood trees, sycamores, and willows, marked the course of some streamlet through a valley. A procession of buffaloes, moving slowly up the profile of one of those distant hills, formed a characteristic object in the savage scene. To the left, the eye stretched beyond this rugged wilderness of hills, and ravines, and ragged forests, to a prairie about ten miles off, extending in a clear blue line along the horizon. It was like looking from among rocks and breakers upon a distant tract of tranquil ocean. Unluckily, our route did not lie in that direction; we still had to traverse many a weary mile of the "cross timber."

We encamped toward evening in a valley, beside a scanty pool, under a scattered grove of elms, the upper branches of which were fringed with tufts of the mystic mistletoe. In the course of the night, the wild colt whinnied repeatedly; and about two hours before day there was a sudden *stampedo*, or rush of horses, along the purlieus of the camp, with a snorting and neighing, and clattering of hoofs, that startled most of the rangers from their sleep, who listened in silence, until the sound died away like the rushing of a blast. As usual, the noise was at first attributed to some party of marauding Indians; but as the day dawned, a couple of wild horses were seen in a neighboring meadow, which scoured off on being approached. It was now supposed that a gang of them had dashed through our camp in the night. A general mustering of our horses took place, many were found scattered to a considerable distance, and several were not to be found. The prints of their hoofs, however, appeared deeply dinted in the soil, leading off at full speed into the waste, and their owners, putting themselves on the trail, set off in weary search of them.

We had a ruddy daybreak, but the morning gathered up gray and lowering, with indications of an autumnal storm. We resumed our march silently and seriously, through a rough and cheerless country, from the highest points of which we could descry large prairies, stretching indefinitely westward. After traveling for two or three hours, as we were traversing a withered prairie, resembling a great brown heath, we beheld seven Osage warriors approaching at a distance. The sight of any human being in this lonely wilderness was interesting; it was like speaking a ship at sea. One of the Indians took the lead of his companions, and advanced toward us with head erect, chest thrown forward, and a free and noble mien. He was a fine-looking fellow, dressed in scarlet frock and fringed leggings of deer skin. His head was decorated with a white tuft, and he stepped forward with something of a martial air, swaying his bow and arrows in one hand.

We held some conversation with him through our interpreter, Beatte, and found that he and his companions had been with the main part of their tribe hunting the buffalo, and had met with great success; and he informed us that, in the course of another day's march, we would reach the prairies on the banks of the Grand Canadian, and find plenty of game. He added that, as their hunt was over, and the hunters on their return homeward, he and his comrades had set out on a war party, to waylay and hover about some Pawnee camp, in hopes of carrying off scalps or horses.

By this time his companions, who at first stood aloof, joined him. Three of them had indifferent fowling-pieces; the rest were armed with bows and arrows. I could not but admire the finely shaped heads and busts of these savages, and their graceful attitudes and expressive gestures, as they stood conversing with our interpreter, and surrounded by a cavalcade of rangers. We endeavored to get one of them to join us, as we were desirous of seeing him hunt the buffalo with his bow and arrow. He seemed at first inclined to do so, but was dissuaded by his companions.

The worthy commissioner now remembered his mission as pacificator, and made a speech, exhorting them to abstain from all offensive acts against the Pawnees; informing them of the plan of their father at Washington, to put an end to all war among his red children; and assuring them that he was sent to the frontier to establish a universal peace. He told them, therefore, to return quietly to their homes, with the certainty that the Pawnees would no longer molest them, but would soon regard them as brothers.

The Indians listened to the speech with their customary silence and decorum; after which, exchanging a few words among themselves, they bade us farewell and pursued their way across the prairie.

Fancying that I saw a lurking smile in the countenance of our interpreter, Beatte, I privately inquired what the Indians had said to each other after hearing the speech. The leader, he said, had observed to his companions that, as their great father intended so soon to put an end to all warfare, it behooved them to make the most of the little time that was left them. So they had departed, with redoubled zeal, to pursue their project of horse stealing!

We had not long parted from the Indians before we discovered three buffaloes among the thickets of a marshy valley to our left. I set off with the captain and several rangers in pursuit of them. Stealing through a straggling grove, the captain, who took the lead, got within rifle-shot, and wounded one of them in the flank. They all three made off in headlong panic, through thickets and brushwood, and swamp and mire, bearing down every obstacle by their immense weight. The captain and rangers soon gave up a chase which threatened to knock up their horses; I had got upon the traces of the wounded bull, however, and was in hopes of getting near enough to use my pistols, the only weapons with which I was provided; but before I could effect it, he reached the foot of a rocky hill, covered with post-oak and brambles, and plunged forward, dashing and crashing along, with neck-or-nothing fury, where it would have been madness to have followed him.

The chase had led me so far on one side that it was some time before I regained the trail of our troop. As I was slowly ascending a hill, a fine black mare came prancing round the summit, and was close to me before she was aware. At sight of me she started back, then turning, swept at full speed down into the valley, and up the opposite hill, with flowing mane and tail, and action free as air. I gazed after her as long as she was in sight, and breathed a wish that so glorious an animal might never come under the degrading thraldom of whip and curb, but remain a free rover of the prairies.

CHAPTER TWENTY-SEVEN

FOUL WEATHER ENCAMPMENT—ANECDOTES OF BEAR HUNTING—INDIAN NOTIONS ABOUT OMENS—SCRUPLES RESPECTING THE DEAD

ON overtaking the troop, I found it encamping in a rich bottom of woodland, traversed by a small stream, running between deep crumbling banks. A sharp cracking off of rifles was kept up for some time in various directions, upon a numerous flock of turkeys, scampering among the thickets or perched upon the trees. We had not been long at a halt when a drizzling rain ushered in the autumnal storm that had been brewing. Preparations were immediately made to weather it; our tent was pitched, and our saddles, saddlebags, packages of coffee, sugar, salt, and everything else that could be damaged by the rain, were gathered under its shelter. Our men, Beatte, Tonish, and Antoine, drove stakes with forked ends into the ground, laid poles across them for rafters, and thus made a shed or pent-house, covered with bark and skins, sloping toward the wind, and open toward the fire. The rangers formed similar shelters of bark and skins, or of blankets stretched on poles, supported by forked stakes, with great fires in front.

These precautions were well timed. The rain set in sullenly and steadily, and kept on, with slight intermissions, for two days. The brook which flowed peacefully on our arrival, swelled into a turbid and boiling torrent, and the forest became little better than a mere swamp. The men gathered under their shelters of skins and blankets, or sat cowering round their fires; while columns of smoke curling up among the trees, and diffusing themselves in the air, spread a blue haze through the woodland. Our poor, wayworn horses, reduced by weary travel and scanty pasturage, lost all remaining spirit, and stood, with drooping heads, flagging ears, and half-closed eyes, dozing and steaming in the rain, while the yellow autumnal leaves, at every shaking of the breeze, came wavering down around them.

Notwithstanding the bad weather, however, our hunters were not idle, but during the intervals of the rain sallied forth on horseback to prowl through the woodland. Every now and then the sharp report of a distant rifle boded the death of a deer. Venison in abundance was brought in. Some busied themselves under the sheds, flaying and cutting up the carcasses, or round the fires with spits and camp kettles, and a rude kind of feasting, or rather gormandizing, prevailed throughout the camp. The ax was continually at work, and wearied the forest with its echoes. Crash! some mighty tree would come down; in a few minutes its limbs would be blazing and crackling on the huge camp fires, with some luckless deer roasting before it that had once sported beneath its shade.

The change of weather had taken sharp hold of our little Frenchman. His meager frame, composed of bones and whipcord, was racked with rheumatic pains and twinges. He had the toothache—the earache—his face was tied up— he had shooting pains in every limb; yet all seemed but to increase his restless activity, and he was an incessant fidget about the fire, roasting, and stewing, and groaning, and scolding, and swearing.

Our man Beatte returned grim and mortified from hunting. He had come upon a bear of formidable dimensions, and wounded him with a rifle-shot. The bear took to the brook, which was swollen and rapid. Beatte dashed after him and assailed him in the rear with his hunting-knife. At every blow the bear turned furiously upon him, with a terrific display of white teeth. Beatte, having a foothold in the brook, was enabled to push him off with his rifle, and, when he turned to swim, would flounder after, and attempt to hamstring him. The bear, however, succeeded in scrambling off among the thickets, and Beatte had to give up the chase.

This adventure, if it produced no game, brought up at least several anecdotes, round the evening fire, relative to bear hunting, in which the grizzly bear figured conspicuously. This powerful and ferocious animal is a favorite theme of hunter's story, both among red and white men; and his enormous claws are worn round the neck of an Indian brave as a trophy more honorable than a human scalp. He is now scarcely seen below the upper prairies and the skirts of the Rocky Mountains. Other bears are formidable when wounded and provoked, but seldom make battle when allowed to escape. The grizzly bear alone, of all the animals of our Western wilds, is prone to unprovoked hostility. His prodigious size and strength make him a formidable opponent; and his great tenacity of life often baffles the skill of the hunter, notwithstanding repeated shots of the rifle, and wounds of the hunting-knife.

One of the anecdotes related on this occasion gave a picture of the accidents and hard shifts to which our frontier rovers are inured. A hunter, while in pursuit of a deer, fell into one of those deep funnel-shaped pits, formed on the prairies by the settling of the waters after heavy rains, and known by the name of sink-holes. To his great horror, he came in contact, at the bottom, with a huge grizzly bear. The monster grappled him; a deadly contest ensued, in which the poor hunter was severely torn and bitten, and had a leg and an arm broken, but succeeded in killing his rugged foe. For several days he remained at the bottom of the pit, too much crippled to move, and subsisting on the raw flesh of the bear, during which time he kept his wounds open, that they might heal gradually and effectually. He was at length enabled to scramble to the top of the pit, and so out upon the open prairie. With great difficulty he crawled to a ravine, formed by a stream, then nearly dry. Here he took a delicious draught of water, which infused new life into him; then dragging himself along from pool to pool, he supported himself by small fish and frogs.

One day he saw a wolf hunt down and kill a deer in the neighboring prairie. He immediately crawled forth from the ravine, drove off the wolf, and, lying down beside the carcass of the deer, remained there until he made several hearty meals, by which his strength was much recruited.

Returning to the ravine, he pursued the course of the brook, until it grew to be a considerable stream. Down this he floated, until he came to where it emptied into the Mississippi. Just at the mouth of the stream he found a forked tree, which he launched with some difficulty, and, getting astride of it, committed himself to the current of the mighty river. In this way he floated along, until he arrived opposite the fort at Council Bluffs. Fortunately he arrived there in the daytime, otherwise he might have floated, unnoticed, past this solitary post, and perished in the idle waste of waters. Being descried from the fort, a canoe was sent to his relief, and he was brought to shore more dead than alive, where he soon recovered from his wounds, but remained maimed for life.

Our man Beatte had come out of his contest with the bear very much worsted and discomfited. His drenching in the brook, together with the recent change of weather, had brought on rheumatic pains in his limbs, to which he is subject. Though ordinarily a fellow of undaunted spirit, and above all hardship, yet he now sat down by the fire, gloomy and dejected, and for once gave way to repining. Though in the prime of life, and of a robust frame and apparently iron constitution, yet, by his own account he was little better than a mere wreck. He was, in fact, a living monument of the hardships of wild frontier life. Baring his left arm, he showed it warped and contracted by a former attack of rheumatism; a malady with which the Indians are often afflicted; for their exposure to the vicissitudes of the

elements does not produce that perfect hardihood and insen-
sibility to the changes of the seasons that many are apt to
imagine. He bore the scars of various maims and bruises;
some received in hunting, some in Indian warfare. His
right arm had been broken by a fall from his horse; at another time his steed had fallen with him, and crushed his
left leg.

"I am all broke to pieces and good for nothing," said he,
"I no care now what happen to me any more. However,"
added he, after a moment's pause, "for all that, it would
take a pretty strong man to put me down, anyhow."

I drew from him various particulars concerning himself,
which served to raise him in my estimation. His residence
was on the Neosho, in an Osage hamlet or neighborhood,
under the superintendence of a worthy missionary from the
banks of the Hudson, by the name of Requa, who was endeavoring to instruct the savages in the art of agriculture,
and to make husbandmen and herdsmen of them. I had
visited this agricultural mission of Requa in the course of
my recent tour along the frontier, and had considered it more
likely to produce solid advantages to the poor Indians than
any of the mere praying and preaching missions along the
border.

In this neighborhood, Pierre Beatte had his little farm,
his Indian wife, and his half-breed children; and aided Mr.
Requa in his endeavors to civilize the habits and meliorate
the condition of the Osage tribe. Beatte had been brought
up a Catholic, and was inflexible in his religious faith; he
could not pray with Mr. Requa, he said, but he could work
with him, and he evinced a zeal for the good of his savage
relations and neighbors. Indeed, though his father had been
French, and he himself had been brought up in communion
with the whites, he evidently was more of an Indian in his
tastes, and his heart yearned toward his mother's nation.
When he talked to me of the wrongs and insults that the
poor Indians suffered in their intercourse with the rough settlers on the frontiers; when he described the precarious and

degraded state of the Osage tribe, diminished in numbers, broken in spirit, and almost living on sufferance in the land where they once figured so heroically, I could see his veins swell, and his nostrils distend with indignation; but he would check the feeling with a strong exertion of Indian self-command, and, in a manner, drive it back into his bosom.

He did not hesitate to relate an instance wherein he had joined his kindred Osages, in pursuing and avenging themselves on a party of white men who had committed a flagrant outrage upon them; and I found, in the encounter that took place, Beatte had shown himself the complete Indian.

He had more than once accompanied his Osage relations in their wars with the Pawnees, and related a skirmish which took place on the borders of these very hunting grounds, in which several Pawnees were killed. We should pass near the place, he said, in the course of our tour, and the unburied bones and skulls of the slain were still to be seen there. The surgeon of the troop, who was present at our conversation, pricked up his ears at this intelligence. He was something of a phrenologist, and offered Beatte a handsome reward if he would procure him one of the skulls.

Beatte regarded him for a moment with a look of stern surprise.

"No!" said he at length, "dat too bad! I have heart strong enough—I no care kill, but *let the dead alone!*"

He added that, once in traveling with a party of white men, he had slept in the same tent with a doctor, and found that he had a Pawnee skull among his baggage: he at once renounced the doctor's tent and his fellowship. "He try to coax me," said Beatte, "but I say no, we must part—I no keep such company."

In the temporary depression of his spirits, Beatte gave way to those superstitious forebodings to which Indians are prone. He had sat for some time, with his cheek upon his hand, gazing into the fire. I found his thoughts were wandering back to his humble home, on the banks of the Neosho; he was sure, he said, that he should find some one of his

family ill or dead on his return: his left eye had twitched
and twinkled for two days past; an omen which always
boded some misfortune of the kind.

Such are the trivial circumstances which, when magnified
into omens, will shake the souls of these men of iron. The
least sign of mystic and sinister portent is sufficient to turn
a hunter or a warrior from his course, or to fill his mind with
apprehensions of impending evil. It is this superstitious propensity, common to the solitary and savage rovers of the
wilderness, that gives such powerful influence to the prophet
and the dreamer.

The Osages, with whom Beatte had passed much of his
life, retain these superstitious fancies and rites in much of
their original force. They all believe in the existence of the
soul after its separation from the body, and that it carries
with it all its mortal tastes and habitudes. At an Osage village in the neighborhood of Beatte, one of the chief warriors
lost an only child, a beautiful girl, of a very tender age. All
her playthings were buried with her. Her favorite little
horse, also, was killed, and laid in the grave beside her, that
she might have it to ride in the land of spirits.

I will here add a little story, which I picked up in the
course of my tour through Beatte's country, and which illus-
trates the superstitions of his Osage kindred. A large party
of Osages had been encamped for some time on the borders
of a fine stream called the Nickanansa. Among them was
a young hunter, one of the bravest and most graceful of the
tribe, who was to be married to an Osage girl, who, for her
beauty, was called the Flower of the Prairies. The young
hunter left her for a time among her relatives in the encampment, and went to St. Louis, to dispose of the products of
his hunting, and purchase ornaments for his bride. After
an absence of some weeks, he returned to the banks of the
Nickanansa, but the camp was no longer there; and the bare
frames of the lodges and the brands of extinguished fires
alone marked the place. At a distance he beheld a female
seated, as if weeping, by the side of the stream. It was his

affianced bride. He ran to embrace her, but she turned mournfully away. He dreaded lest some evil had befallen the camp.

"Where are our people?" cried he.

"They are gone to the banks of the Wagrushka."

"And what art thou doing here alone?"

"Waiting for thee."

"Then let us hasten to join our people on the banks of the Wagrushka."

He gave her his pack to carry, and walked ahead, according to the Indian custom.

They came to where the smoke of the distant camp was seen rising from the woody margin of the stream. The girl seated herself at the foot of a tree. "It is not proper for us to return together," said she; "I will wait here."

The young hunter proceeded to the camp alone, and was received by his relations with gloomy countenances.

"What evil has happened," said he, "that ye are all so sad?"

No one replied.

He turned to his favorite sister, and bade her go forth, seek his bride, and conduct her to the camp.

"Alas!" cried she, "how shall I seek her? She died a few days since."

The relations of the young girl now surrounded him, weeping and wailing; but he refused to believe the dismal tidings. "But a few moments since," cried he, "I left her alone and in health: come with me, and I will conduct you to her."

He led the way to the tree where she had seated herself, but she was no longer there, and his pack lay on the ground. The fatal truth struck him to the heart; he fell to the ground dead.

I give this simple story almost in the words in which it was related to me, as I lay by the fire in an evening encampment on the banks of the haunted stream where it is said to have happened.

CHAPTER TWENTY-EIGHT

A SECRET EXPEDITION—DEER BLEATING—MAGIC BALLS

ON the following morning we were rejoined by the rangers who had remained at the last encampment to seek for the stray horses. They had tracked them for a considerable distance through bush and brake, and across streams, until they found them crooping the herbage on the edge of a prairie. Their heads were in the direction of the fort, and they were evidently grazing their way homeward, heedless of the unbounded freedom of the prairie so suddenly laid open to them.

About noon the weather held up, and I observed a mysterious consultation going on between our half-breeds and Tonish; it ended in a request that we would dispense with the services of the latter for a few hours, and permit him to join his comrades in a grand foray. We objected that Tonish was too much disabled by aches and pains for such an undertaking; but he was wild with eagerness for the mysterious enterprise, and, when permission was given him, seemed to forget all his ailments in an instant.

In a short time the trio were equipped and on horseback; with rifles on their shoulders and handkerchiefs twisted round their heads, evidently bound for a grand scamper. As they passed by the different lodges of the camp, the vainglorious little Frenchman could not help boasting to the right and left of the great things he was about to achieve; though the taciturn Beatte, who rode in advance, would every now and then check his horse, and look back at him with an air of stern rebuke. It was hard, however, to make the loquacious Tonish play "Indian."

Several of the hunters, likewise, sallied forth, and the

prime old woodman, Ryan, came back early in the afternoon, with ample spoil, having killed a buck and two fat does. I drew near to a group of rangers that had gathered round him as he stood by the spoil, and found they were discussing the merits of a stratagem sometimes used in deer hunting. This consists in imitating, with a small instrument called a bleat, the cry of the fawn, so as to lure the doe within reach of the rifle. There are bleats of various kinds, suited to calm or windy weather, and to the age of the fawn. The poor animal, deluded by them, in its anxiety about its young, will sometimes advance close up to the hunter. "I once bleated a doe," said a young hunter, "until it came within twenty yards of me, and presented a sure mark. I leveled my rifle three times, but had not the heart to shoot, for the poor doe looked so wistfully that it in a manner made my heart yearn. I thought of my own mother, and how anxious she used to be about me when I was a child; so to put an end to the matter, I gave a halloo, and started the doe out of rifle-shot in a moment."

"And you did right," cried honest old Ryan. "For my part, I never could bring myself to bleating deer. I've been with hunters who had bleats, and have made them throw them away. It is a rascally trick to take advantage of a mother's love for her young."

Toward evening our three worthies returned from their mysterious foray. The tongue of Tonish gave notice of their approach long before they came in sight; for he was vociferating at the top of his lungs, and rousing the attention of the whole camp. The lagging gait and reeking flanks of their horses gave evidence of hard riding; and, on nearer approach, we found them hung round with meat like a butcher's shambles. In fact, they had been scouring an immense prairie that extended beyond the forest, and which was covered with herds of buffalo. Of this prairie, and the animals upon it, Beatte had received intelligence a few days before, in his conversation with the Osages, but had kept the information a secret from the rangers, that he and his comrades might have the first dash at the game. They had contented themselves with killing four; though, if Tonish might be believed, they might have slain them by scores.

These tidings, and the buffalo meat brought home in evidence, spread exultation through the camp, and every one looked forward with joy to a buffalo hunt on the prairies. Tonish was again the oracle of the camp, and held forth by the hour to a knot of listeners, crouched round the fire, with their shoulders up to their ears. He was now more boastful than ever of his skill as a marksman. All his want of suc cess in the early part of our march he attributed to being "out of luck," if not "spellbound"; and finding himself listened to with apparent credulity, gave an instance of the kind, which he declared had happened to himself, but which was evidently a tale picked up among his relations, the Osages.

According to this account, when about fourteen years of age, as he was one day hunting, he saw a white deer come out from a ravine. Crawling near to get a shot, he beheld another and another come forth, until there were seven, all as white as snow. Having crept sufficiently near, he singled one out and fired, but without effect; the deer remained unfrightened. He loaded and fired again and missed. Thus he continued firing and missing until all his ammunition was expended, and the deer remained without a wound. He re turned home despairing of his skill as a marksman, but was consoled by an old Osage hunter. These white deer, said he, have a charmed life,. and can only be killed by bullets of a particular kind.

The old Indian cast several balls for Tonish, but would not suffer him to be present on the occasion, nor inform him of the ingredients and mystic ceremonials.

Provided with these balls, Tonish again set out in quest of the white deer, and succeeded in finding them. He tried at first with ordinary balls, but missed as before. A magic ball, however, immediately brought a fine buck to the ground. Whereupon the rest of the herd immediately disappeared and were never seen again.

October 29th.—The morning opened gloomy and lowering; but toward eight o'clock the sun struggled forth and lighted up the forest, and the notes of the bugle gave signal to prepare for marching. Now began a scene of bustle, and clamor, and gayety. Some were scampering and brawling after their horses, some were riding in bare-backed and driving in the horses of their comrades. Some were stripping the poles of the wet blankets that had served for shelters; others packing up with all possible dispatch, and loading the baggage horses as they arrived, while others were cracking off their damp rifles and charging them afresh, to be ready for the sport.

About ten o'clock we began our march. I loitered in the rear of the troop as it forded the turbid brook, and defiled through the labyrinths of the forest. I always felt disposed to linger until the last straggler disappeared among the trees and the distant note of the bugle died upon the ear, that I might behold the wilderness relapsing into silence and solitude. In the present instance, the deserted scene of our late bustling encampment had a forlorn and desolate appearance. The surrounding forest had been in many places trampled into a quagmire. Trees felled and partly hewn in pieces, and scattered in huge fragments; tent-poles stripped of their covering; smoldering fires, with great morsels of roasted venison and buffalo meat, standing in wooden spits before them, hacked and slashed by the knives of hungry hunters; while around were strewed the hides, the horns, the antlers, and bones of buffaloes and deer, with uncooked joints, and unplucked turkeys, left behind with that reckless improvidence and wastefulness which young hunters are apt to indulge when in a neighborhood where game abounds. In the meantime a score or two of turkey-buzzards or vultures were already on the wing, wheeling their magnificent flight high in the high, and preparing for a descent upon the camp as soon as it should be abandoned.

CHAPTER TWENTY-NINE

THE GRAND PRAIRIE—A BUFFALO HUNT

AFTER proceeding about two hours in a southerly direction, we emerged toward midday from the dreary belt of the Cross Timber, and to our infinite delight beheld "the great Prairie" stretching to the right and left before us. We could distinctly trace the meandering course of the main Canadian, and various smaller streams, by the strips of green forest that bordered them. The landscape was vast and beautiful. There is always an expansion of feeling in looking upon these boundless and fertile wastes; but I was doubly conscious of it after emerging from our "close dungeon of innumerous boughs."

From a rising ground Beatte pointed out the place where he and his comrades had killed the buffaloes; and we beheld several black objects moving in the distance, which he said were part of the herd. The captain determined to shape his course to a woody bottom about a mile distant, and to encamp there for a day or two, by way of having a regular buffalo hunt, and getting a supply of provisions. As the troop defiled along the slope of the hill toward the camping ground, Beatte proposed to my messmates and myself that we should put ourselves under his guidance, promising to take us where we should have plenty of sport. Leaving the line of march, therefore, we diverged toward the prairie; traversing a small valley, and ascending a gentle swell of land. As we reached the summit, we beheld a gang of wild horses about a mile off. Beatte was immediately on the alert, and no longer thought of buffalo hunting. He was mounted on his powerful half-wild horse, with a lariat coiled at the saddle-bow, and set off in pursuit; while we remained on a rising ground watching his maneuvers with great solicitude. Taking advantage of a strip of woodland, he stole quietly along, so as to get close to them before he was perceived. The moment they caught sight of him a grand scamper took place. We watched him skirting along the horizon like a privateer in full chase of a merchantman; at length he passed over the brow of a ridge and down into a shallow valley; in a few moments he was on the opposite hill, and close upon one of the horses. He was soon head and head, and appeared to be trying to noose his prey; but they both disappeared again below the hill, and we saw no more of them. It turned out afterward that he had noosed a powerful horse, but could not hold him, and had lost his lariat in the attempt.

While we were waiting for his return, we perceived two buffalo bulls descending a slope, toward a stream, which wound through a ravine fringed with trees. The young count and myself endeavored to get near them under covert of the trees. They discovered us while we were yet three or four hundred yards off, and, turning about, retreated up the rising ground. We urged our horses across the ravine and gave chase. The immense weight of head and shoulders causes the buffalo to labor heavily up hill; but it accelerates his descent. We had the advantage, therefore, and gained rapidly upon the fugitives, though it was difficult to get our horses to approach them, their very scent inspiring them with terror. The count, who had a double-barreled gun, loaded with ball, fired, but it missed. The bulls now altered their course, and galloped down hill with headlong rapidity. As they ran in different directions, we each singled out one and separated. I was provided with a brace of veteran brass-barreled pistols, which I had borrowed at Fort Gibson, and which had evidently seen some service. Pistols are very effective in buffalo hunting, as the hunter can ride up close to the animal, and fire at it while at full speed; whereas the long heavy rifles used on the frontier cannot be easily managed, nor discharged with accurate aim from horseback.

My object, therefore, was to get within pistol shot of the buffalo. This was no very easy matter. I was well mounted on a horse of excellent speed and bottom, that seemed eager for the chase, and soon overtook the game; but the moment he came nearly parallel, he would keep sheering off, with ears forked and pricked forward, and every symptom of aversion and alarm. It was no wonder. Of all animals, a buffalo, when close pressed by the hunter, has an aspect the most diabolical. His two short black horns curve out of a huge frontier of shaggy hair; his eyes glow like coals; his mouth is open, his tongue parched and drawn up into a half crescent; his tail is erect, and tufted and whisking about in the air. He is a perfect picture of mingled rage and terror.

It was with difficulty I urged my horse sufficiently near, when, taking aim, to my chagrin, both pistols missed fire. Unfortunately the locks of these veteran weapons were so much worn that, in the gallop, the priming had been shaken out of the pans. At the snapping of the last pistol I was close upon the buffalo, when, in his despair, he turned round with a sudden snort and rushed upon me. My horse wheeled about as if on a pivot, made a convulsive spring, and, as I had been leaning on one side with pistol extended, I came near being thrown at the feet of the buffalo.

Three or four bounds of the horse carried us out of the reach of the enemy; who, having merely turned in desperate self-defense, quickly resumed his flight. As soon as I could gather in my panic-stricken horse, and prime the pistols afresh, I again spurred in pursuit of the buffalo, who had slackened his speed to take breath. On my approach he again set off full tilt, heaving himself forward with a heavy rolling gallop, dashing with headlong precipitation through brakes and ravines, while several deer and wolves, startled from their coverts by his thundering career, ran helter-skelter to right and left across the waste.

A gallop across the prairies in pursuit of game is by no means so smooth a career as those may imagine who have only the idea of an open level plain. It is true, the prairies of the hunting ground are not so much entangled with flowering plants and long herbage as the lower prairies, and are principally covered with short buffalo grass; but they are diversified by hill and dale, and where most level are apt to be cut up by deep rifts and ravines, made by torrents after rains; and which, yawning from an even surface, are almost like pitfalls in the way of the hunter, checking him suddenly, when in full career, or subjecting him to the risk of limb and life. The plains, too, are beset by burrowing holes of small animals, in which the horse is apt to sink to the fetlock and throw both himself and his rider. The late rain had covered some parts of the prairie, where the ground was hard, with a thin sheet of water, through which the horse had to splash his way. In other parts there were innumerable shallow hollows, eight or ten feet in diameter, made by the buffaloes, who wallow in sand and mud like swine. These being filled with water, shone like mirrors, so that the horse was continually leaping over them or springing on one side. We had reached, too, a rough part of the prairie, very much broken and cut up; the buffalo, who was running for life, took no heed to his course, plunging down break-neck ravines, where it was necessary to skirt the borders in search of a safer descent. At length we came to where a winter stream had torn a deep chasm across the whole prairie, leaving open jagged rocks, and forming a long glen bordered by steep crumbling cliffs of mingled stone and clay. Down one of these the buffalo flung himself, half tumbling, half leaping, and then scuttled along the bottom; while I, seeing all further pursuit useless, pulled up, and gazed quietly after him from the border of the cliff, until he disappeared amid the windings of the ravine.

Nothing now remained but to turn my steed and rejoin my companions. Here at first was some little difficulty. The ardor of the chase had betrayed me into a long, heedless gallop. I now found myself in the midst of a lonely waste, in which the prospect was bounded by undulating swells of land, naked and uniform, where, from the deficiency of landmarks and distinct features, an inexperienced man may become bewildered, and lose his way as readily as in the wastes of the ocean. The day, too, was overcast, so that I could not guide myself by the sun; my only mode was to retrace the track my horse had made in coming, though this I would often lose sight of where the ground was covered with parched herbage.

To one unaccustomed to it, there is something inexpressibly lonely in the solitude of a prairie. The loneliness of a forest seems nothing to it. There the view is shut in by trees, and the imagination is left free to picture some livelier scene beyond. But here we have an immense extent of landscape without a sign of human existence. We have the consciousness of being far, far beyond the bounds of human habitation; we feel as if moving in the midst of a desert world. As my horse lagged slowly back over the scenes of our late scamper, and the delirium of the chase had passed away, I was peculiarly sensible to these circumstances. The silence of the waste was now and then broken by the cry of a distant flock of pelicans, stalking like specters about a shallow pool; sometimes by the sinister croaking of a raven in the air, while occasionally a scoundrel wolf would scour off from before me; and, having attained a safe distance, would sit down and howl and whine with tones that gave a dreariness to the surrounding solitude.

After pursuing my way for some time, I descried a horseman on the edge of a distant hill, and soon recognized him to be the count. He had been equally unsuccessful with myself; we were shortly after rejoined by our worthy comrade, the Virtuoso, who, with spectacles on nose, had made two or three ineffectual shots from horseback.

We determined not to seek the camp until we had made one more effort. Casting our eyes about the surrounding waste, we descried a herd of buffalo about two miles distant, scattered apart, and quietly grazing near a small strip of trees and bushes. It required but little stretch of fancy to picture them so many cattle grazing on the edge of a common, and that the grove might shelter some lowly farmhouse.

We now formed our plan to circumvent the herd, and by getting on the other side of them, to hunt them in the direction where we knew our camp to be situated, otherwise the pursuit might take us to such a distance as to render it impossible to find our way back before nightfall. Taking a wide circuit, therefore, we moved slowly and cautiously, pausing occasionally, when we saw any of the herd desist from grazing. The wind fortunately set from them, otherwise they might have scented us and have taken the alarm. In this way we succeeded in getting round the herd without disturbing it. It consisted of about forty head, bulls, cows, and calves. Separating to some distance from each other, we now approached slowly in a parallel line, hoping by degrees to steal near without exciting attention. They began, however, to move off quietly, stopping at every step or two to graze, when suddenly a bull that, unobserved by us, had been taking his siesta under a clump of trees to our left, roused himself from his lair, and hastened to join his companions. We were still at a considerable distance, but the game had taken the alarm. We quickened our pace, they broke into a gallop, and now commenced a full chase.

As the ground was level, they shouldered along with great speed, following each other in a line; two or three bulls bringing up the rear, the last of whom, from his enormous size and venerable frontlet, and beard of sunburned hair, looked like the patriarch of the herd; and as if he might long have reigned the monarch of the prairie.

There is a mixture of the awful and the comic in the look of these huge animals, as they bear their great bulk forward, with an up and down motion of the unwieldy head and shoulders; their tail cocked up like the queue of Pantaloon in a pantomime, the end whisking about in a fierce yet whimsical style, and their eyes glaring venomously with an expression of fright and fury.

For some time I kept parallel with the line, without being

able to force my horse within pistol shot, so much had he been alarmed by the assault of the buffalo in the preceding chase. At length I succeeded, but was again balked by my pistols missing fire. My companions, whose horses were less fleet, and more way-worn, could not overtake the herd; at length Mr. L., who was in the rear of the line, and losing ground, leveled his double-barreled gun, and fired a long raking shot. It struck a buffalo just above the loins, broke its backbone, and brought it to the ground. He stopped and alighted to dispatch his prey; when, borrowing his gun, which had yet a charge remaining in it, I put my horse to its speed, again overtook the herd which was thundering along, pursued by the count. With my present weapon there was no need of urging my horse to such close quarters; galloping along parallel, therefore, I singled out a buffalo, and by a fortunate shot brought it down on the spot. The ball had struck a vital part; it could not move from the place where it fell, but lay there struggling in mortal agony, while the rest of the herd kept on their headlong career across the prairie.

Dismounting, I now fettered my horse to prevent his straying, and advanced to contemplate my victim. I am nothing of a sportsman; I had been prompted to this unwonted exploit by the magnitude of the game and the excitement of an adventurous chase. Now that the excitement was over, I could not but look with commiseration upon the poor animal that lay struggling and bleeding at my feet. His very size and importance, which had before inspired me with eagerness, now increased my compunction. It seemed as if I had inflicted pain in proportion to the bulk of my victim, and as if it were a hundred-fold greater waste of life than there would have been in the destruction of an animal of inferior size.

To add to these after-qualms of conscience, the poor animal lingered in his agony. He had evidently received a mortal wound, but death might be long in coming. It would not do to leave him here to be torn piecemeal, while yet alive,

by the wolves that had already snuffed his blood, and were
skulking and howling at a distance, and waiting for my departure; and by the ravens that were flapping about, croaking dismally in the air. It became now an act of mercy to
give him his quietus, and put him out of his misery. I
primed one of the pistols, therefore, and advanced close up
to the buffalo. To inflict a wound thus in cold blood, I
found a totally different thing from firing in the heat of the
chase. Taking aim, however, just behind the foreshoulder,
my pistol for once proved true; the ball must have passed
through the heart, for the animal gave one convulsive throe
and expired.

While I stood meditating and moralizing over the wreck
I had so wantonly produced, with my horse grazing near
me, I was rejoined by my fellow-sportsman, the Virtuoso;
who, being a man of universal adroitness, and withal more
experienced and hardened in the gentle art of "venerie,"
soon managed to carve out the tongue of the buffalo, and
delivered it to me to bear back to the camp as a trophy.

CHAPTER THIRTY

A COMRADE LOST—A SEARCH FOR THE CAMP—THE COM-
MISSIONER, THE WILD HORSE, AND THE BUFFALO—
A WOLF SERENADE

OUR solicitude was now awakened for the young count.
With his usual eagerness and impetuosity he had persisted
in urging his jaded horse in pursuit of the herd, unwilling to
return without having likewise killed a buffalo. In this way
he had kept on following them, hither and thither, and occasionally firing an ineffectual shot, until by degrees horseman
and herd became indistinct in the distance, and at length
swelling ground and strips of trees and thickets hid them
entirely from sight.

By the time my friend, the amateur, joined me, the young

count had been long lost to view. We held a consultation on the matter. Evening was drawing on. Were we to pursue him, it would be dark before we should overtake him, granting we did not entirely lose trace of him in the gloom. We should then be too much bewildered to find our way back to the encampment; even now, our return would be difficult. We determined, therefore, to hasten to the camp as speedily as possible, and send out our half-breeds, and some of the veteran hunters, skilled in cruising about the prairies, to search for our companion.

We accordingly set forward in what we supposed to be the direction of the camp. Our weary horses could hardly be urged beyond a walk. The twilight thickened upon us; the landscape grew gradually indistinct; we tried in vain to recognize various landmarks which we had noted in the morning. The features of the prairies are so similar as to baffle the eye of any but an Indian, or a practiced woodman. At length night closed in. We hoped to see the distant glare of camp-fires; we listened to catch the sound of the bells about the necks of the grazing horses. Once or twice we thought we distinguished them; we were mistaken. Nothing was to be heard but a monotonous concert of insects, with now and then the dismal howl of wolves mingling with the night breeze. We began to think of halting for the night, and bivouacking under the lee of some thicket. We had implements to strike a light; there was plenty of firewood at hand, and the tongues of our buffaloes would furnish us with a repast.

Just as we were preparing to dismount, we heard the report of a rifle, and shortly after the notes of the bugle calling up the night guard. Pushing forward in that direction, the camp fires soon broke on our sight, gleaming at a distance from among the thick groves of an alluvial bottom.

As we entered the camp, we found it a scene of rude hunters' revelry and wassail. There had been a grand day's sport, in which all had taken a part. Eight buffaloes had been killed; roaring fires were blazing on every side; all hands were feasting upon roasted joints, broiled marrow-bones, and the juicy hump, far-famed among the epicures of the prairies. Right glad were we to dismount and partake of the sturdy cheer, for we had been on our weary horses since morning without tasting food.

As to our worthy friend, the commissioner, with whom we had parted company at the outset of this eventful day, we found him lying in a corner of the tent, much the worse for wear, in the course of a successful hunting match.

It seems that our man, Beatte, in his zeal to give the commissioner an opportunity of distinguishing himself, and gratifying his hunting propensities, had mounted him upon his half-wild horse, and started him in pursuit of a huge buffalo bull, that had already been frightened by the hunters. The horse, which was fearless as his owner, and, like him, had a considerable spice of devil in his composition, and who, besides, had been made familiar with the game, no sooner came in sight and scent of the buffalo than he set off full speed, bearing the involuntary hunter hither and thither, and whither he would not—up hill and down hill—leaping pools and brooks—dashing through glens and gullies, until he came up with the game. Instead of sheering off, he crowded upon the buffalo. The commissioner, almost in self-defense, discharged both barrels of a double-barreled gun into the enemy. The broadside took effect, but was not mortal. The buffalo turned furiously upon his pursuer; the horse, as he had been taught by his owner, wheeled off. The buffalo plunged after him. The worthy commissioner, in great extremity, drew his sole pistol from his holster, fired it off as a stern-chaser, shot the buffalo full in the breast, and brought him lumbering forward to the earth.

The commissioner returned to camp, lauded on all sides for his signal exploit; but grievously battered and way-worn. He had been a hard rider perforce, and a victor in spite of himself. He turned a deaf ear to all compliments and con-gratulations; had but little stomach for the hunter's fare placed before him, and soon retreated to stretch his limbs in the tent, declaring that nothing should tempt him again to mount that half devil Indian horse, and that he had had enough buffalo hunting for the rest of his life.

It was too dark now to send any one in search of the young count. Guns, however, were fired, and the bugle sounded from time to time, to guide him to the camp, if by chance he should straggle within hearing; but the night advanced without his making his appearance. There was not a star visible to guide him, and we concluded that wherever he was he would give up wandering in the dark and bivouac until daybreak.

It was a raw, overcast night. The carcasses of the buffaloes killed in the vicinity of the camp had drawn about it an unusual number of wolves, who kept up the most forlorn concert of whining yells, prolonged into dismal cadences and inflexions, literally converting the surrounding waste into a howling wilderness. Nothing is more melancholy than the midnight howl of a wolf on a prairie. What rendered the gloom and wildness of the night and the savage concert of the neighboring waste the more dreary to us was the idea of the lonely and exposed situation of our young and inexperienced comrade. We trusted, however, that on the return of daylight, he would find his way back to the camp, and then all the events of the night would be remembered only as so many savory gratifications of his passion for adventure.

CHAPTER THIRTY-ONE

A HUNT FOR A LOST COMRADE

THE morning dawned, and an hour or two passed without any tidings of the count. We began to feel uneasiness lest, having no compass to aid him, he might perplex himself and wander in some opposite direction. Stragglers are thus often lost for days; what made us the more anxious about him was, that he had no provisions with him, was totally unversed in "wood craft," and liable to fall into the hands of some lurking or straggling party of savages.

As soon as our people, therefore, had made their breakfast, we beat up for volunteers for a cruise in search of the count. A dozen of the rangers, mounted on some of the best and freshest horses, and armed with rifles, were soon ready to start; our half-breeds Beatte and Antoine also, with our little mongrel Frenchman, were zealous in the cause; so Mr. L. and myself taking the lead, to show the way to the scene of our little hunt where we had parted company with the count, we all set out across the prairie. A ride of a couple of miles brought us to the carcasses of the two buffaloes we had killed. A legion of ravenous wolves were already gorging upon them. At our approach they reluctantly drew off, skulking with a caitiff look to the distance of a few hundred yards, and there awaiting our departure, that they might return to their banquet.

I conducted Beatte and Antoine to the spot whence the young count had continued the chase alone. It was like putting hounds upon the scent. They immediately distinguished the track of his horse amid the trampings of the buffaloes, and set off at a round pace, following with the eye in nearly a straight course, for upward of a mile, when they came to where the herd had divided, and run hither and thither about a meadow. Here the track of the horse's hoofs wandered and doubled and often crossed each other; our half-breeds were like hounds at fault. While we were at a halt, waiting until they should unravel the maze, Beatte suddenly gave a short Indian whoop, or rather yelp, and pointed to a distant hill. On regarding it attentively, we perceived a horseman on the summit. "It is the count!" cried Beatte, and set off at full gallop, followed by the whole company. In a few moments he checked his horse. Another figure on horseback had appeared on the brow of the hill. This completely altered the case. The count had wandered off alone; no other person had been missing from the camp. If

one of these horsemen were indeed the count, the other must
be an Indian. If an Indian, in all probability a Pawnee.
Perhaps they were both Indians; scouts of some party lurking in the vicinity. While these and other suggestions were
hastily discussed, the two horsemen glided down from the
profile of the hill, and we lost sight of them. One of the
rangers suggested that there might be a straggling party of
Pawnees behind the hill, and that the count might have
fallen into their hands. The idea had an electric effect upon
the little troop. In an instant every horse was at full speed
the half-breeds leading the way; the young rangers as they
rode set up wild yelps of exultation at the thoughts of having
a brush with the Indians. A neck or nothing gallop brought
us to the skirts of the hill and revealed our mistake. In a
ravine we found the two horsemen standing by the carcass
of a buffalo which they had killed. They proved to be two
rangers, who, unperceived, had left the camp a little before
us, and had come here in a direct line, while we had made
a wide circuit about the prairie.

This episode being at an end, and the sudden excitement
being over, we slowly and coolly retraced our steps to the
meadow; but it was some time before our half-breeds could
again get on the track of the count. Having at length found
it, they succeeded in following it through all its doublings,
until they came to where it was no longer mingled with the
tramp of buffaloes, but became single and separate, wandering here and there about the prairies, but always tending in
a direction opposite to that of the camp. Here the count had
evidently given up the pursuit of the herd, and had endeavored to find his way to the encampment, but had become
bewildered as the evening shades thickened around him, and
had completely mistaken the points of the compass.

In all this quest our half-breeds displayed that quickness
of eye, in following up a track, for which Indians are so
noted. Beatte, especially, was as stanch as a veteran hound.
Sometimes he would keep forward on an easy trot; his eyes
fixed on the ground a little ahead of his horse, clearly dis-

tinguishing prints in the herbage which to me were invisible, excepting on the closest inspection. Sometimes he would pull up and walk his horse slowly, regarding the ground intensely, where to my eye nothing was apparent. Then he would dismount, lead his horse by the bridle, and advance cautiously step by step, with his face bent toward the earth, just catching, here and there, a casual indication of the vaguest kind to guide him onward. In some places where the soil was hard and the grass withered he would lose the track entirely, and wander backward and forward, and right and left, in search of it; returning occasionally to the place where he had lost sight of it, to take a new departure. If this failed he would examine the banks of the neighboring streams, or the sandy bottoms of the ravines, in hopes of finding tracks where the count had crossed. When he again came upon the track, he would remount his horse and resume his onward course. At length, after crossing a stream, in the crumbling banks of which the hoofs of the horse were deeply dented, we came upon a high dry prairie, where our half-breeds were completely baffled. Not a footprint was to be discerned, though they searched in every direction; and Beatte, at length coming to a pause, shook his head despondingly.

Just then a small herd of deer, roused from a neighboring ravine, came bounding by us. Beatte sprang from his horse, leveled his rifle, and wounded one slightly, but without bringing it to the ground. The report of the rifle was almost immediately followed by a long halloo from a distance. We looked around but could see nothing. Another long halloo was heard, and at length a horseman was descried emerging out of a skirt of forest. A single glance showed him to be the young count; there was a universal shout and scamper, every one setting off full gallop to greet him. It was a joyful meeting to both parties; for much anxiety had been felt by us all on account of his youth and inexperience, and for his part, with all his love of adventure, he seemed right glad to be once more among his friends.

* * * 22—VOL. VII.

As we supposed, he had completely mistaken his course on the preceding evening, and had wandered about until dark, when he thought of bivouacking. The night was cold, yet he feared to make a fire, lest it might betray him to some lurking party of Indians. Hobbling his horse with his pocket-handkerchief, and leaving him to graze on the margin of the prairie, he clambered into a tree, fixed his saddle in the fork of the branches, and placing himself securely with his back against the trunk, prepared to pass a dreary and anxious night, regaled occasionally with the howlings of the wolves. He was agreeably disappointed. The fatigue of the day soon brought on a sound sleep; he had delightful dreams about his home in Switzerland, nor did he wake until it was broad daylight.

He then descended from his roosting-place, mounted his horse, and rode to the naked summit of a hill, whence he beheld a trackless wilderness around him, but, at no great distance, the Grand Canadian, winding its way between borders of forest land. The sight of this river consoled him with the idea that, should he fail in finding his way back to the camp, or in being found by some party of his comrades, he might follow the course of the stream, which could not fail to conduct him to some frontier post or Indian hamlet. So closed the events of our haphazard buffalo hunt.

CHAPTER THIRTY-TWO

A REPUBLIC OF PRAIRIE DOGS

On returning from our expedition in quest of the young count, I learned that a burrow, or village, as it is termed, of prairie dogs had been discovered on the level summit of a hill, about a mile from the camp. Having heard much of the habits and peculiarities of these little animals, I determined to pay a visit to the community. The prairie dog is, in fact, one of the curiosities of the Far West, about which travelers delight to tell marvelous tales, endowing him at times with something of the politic and social habits of a rational being, and giving him systems of civil government and domestic economy, almost equal to what they used to bestow upon the beaver.

The prairie dog is an animal of the coney kind, and about the size of a rabbit. He is of a sprightly mercurial nature; quick, sensitive, and somewhat petulant. He is very gregarious, living in large communities, sometimes of several acres in extent, where innumerable little heaps of earth show the entrances to the subterranean cells of the inhabitants, and the well beaten tracks, like lanes and streets, show their mobility and restlessness. According to the accounts given of them, they would seem to be continually full of sport, business, and public affairs; whisking about hither and thither, as if on gossiping visits to each other's houses, or congregating in the cool of the evening, or after a shower, and gamboling together in the open air. Sometimes, especially when the moon shines, they pass half the night in revelry, barking or yelping with short, quick, yet weak tones, like those of very young puppies. While in the height of their playfulness and clamor, however, should there be the least alarm, they all vanish into their cells in an instant, and the village remains blank and silent. In case they are hard pressed by their pursuers, without any hope of escape, they will assume a pugnacious air and a most whimsical look of impotent wrath and defiance.

The prairie dogs are not permitted to remain sole and undisturbed inhabitants of their own homes. Owls and rattlesnakes are said to take up their abodes with them; but whether as invited guests or unwelcome intruders is a matter of controversy. The owls are of a peculiar kind, and would seem to partake of the character of the hawk; for they are taller and more erect on their legs, more alert in their looks and rapid in their flight than ordinary owls, and do not confine their excursions to the night, but sally forth in broad day.

Some say that they only inhabit cells which the prairie dogs have deserted, and suffered to go to ruin, in consequence of the death in them of some relative; for they would make out this little animal to be endowed with keen sensibilities, that will not permit it to remain in the dwelling where it has witnessed the death of a friend. Other fanciful speculators represent the owl as a kind of housekeeper to the prairie dog; and, from having a note very similar, insinuate that it acts, in a manner, as family preceptor, and teaches the young litter to bark.

As to the rattlesnake, nothing satisfactory has been as certained of the part he plays in this most interesting household; though he is considered as little better than a sycophant and sharper, that winds himself into the concerns of the honest, credulous little dog, and takes him in most sadly. Certain it is, if he acts as toad-eater, he occasionally solaces himself with more than the usual perquisities of his order; as he is now and then detected with one of the younger members of the family in his maw.

Such are a few of the particulars that I could gather about the domestic economy of this little inhabitant of the prairies, who, with his pigmy republic, appears to be a subject of much whimsical speculation and burlesque remarks among the hunters of the Far West.

It was toward evening that I set out with a companion, to visit the village in question. Unluckily, it had been in vaded in the course of the day by some of the rangers, who had shot two or three of its inhabitants, and thrown the whole sensitive community in confusion. As we approached we could perceive numbers of the inhabitants seated at the entrances of their cells, while sentinels seemed to have been posted on the outskirts to keep a lookout. At sight of us, the picket guards scampered in and gave the alarm; whereupon every inhabitant gave a short yelp, or bark, and dived into his hole, his heels twinkling in the air as if he had thrown a somersault.

We traversed the whole village, or republic, which covered an area of about thirty acres; but not a whisker of an inhabitant was to be seen. We probed their cells as far as the ramrods of our rifles would reach, but could unearth neither dog, nor owl, nor rattlesnake. Moving quietly to a little distance, we lay down upon the ground, and watched for a long time silent and motionless. By and by, a cautious old burgher would slowly put forth the end of his nose, but instantly draw it in again. Another, at a greater distance, would emerge entirely; but, catching a glance of us, would throw a somersault and plunge back again into his hole. At length, some who resided on the opposite side of the village, taking courage from the continued stillness, would steal forth, and hurry off to a distant hole, the residence possibly of some family connection, or gossiping friend, about whose safety they were solicitous, or with whom they wished to compare notes about the late occurrences.

Others, still more bold, assembled in little knots, in the streets and public places, as if to discuss the recent outrages offered to the commonwealth, and the atrocious murders of their fellow-burghers.

We rose from the ground and moved forward, to take a nearer view of these public proceedings, when yelp! yelp! yelp!—there was a shrill alarm passed from mouth to mouth; the meetings suddenly dispersed; feet twinkled in the air in every direction; and in an instant all had vanished into the earth.

The dusk of the evening put an end to our observations, but the train of whimsical comparisons produced in my brain by the moral attributes which I had heard given to these little politic animals, still continued after my return to camp; and late in the night, as I lay awake after all the camp was asleep, and heard in the stillness of the hour, a faint clamor of shrill voices from the distant village, I could not help picturing to myself the inhabitants gathered together in noisy assemblage and windy debate, to devise plans for the public safety, and to vindicate the invaded rights and insulted dignity of the republic.

CHAPTER THIRTY-THREE

A COUNCIL IN THE CAMP—REASONS FOR FACING HOME-
WARD—HORSES LOST — DEPARTURE WITH A DETACH-
MENT ON THE HOMEWARD ROUTE—SWAMP—WILD HORSE
—CAMP SCENES BY NIGHT—THE OWL, HARBINGER OF
DAWN

WHILE breakfast was preparing, a council was held as to
our future movements. Symptoms of discontent had appeared for a day or two past among the rangers, most of
whom, unaccustomed to the life of the prairies, had become
impatient of its privations, as well as the restraints of the
camp. The want of bread had been felt severely, and they
were wearied with constant travel. In fact, the novelty and
excitement of the expedition were at an end. They had
hunted the deer, the bear, the elk, the buffalo, and the wild
horse, and had no further object of leading interest to look
forward to. A general inclination prevailed, therefore, to
turn homeward.

Grave reasons disposed the captain and his officers to
adopt this resolution. Our horses were generally much
jaded by the fatigues of traveling and hunting, and had
fallen away sadly for want of good pasturage, and from
being tethered at night, to be protected from Indian depredations. The late rains, too, seemed to have washed
away the nourishment from the scanty herbage that remained; and since our encampment during the storm, our
horses had lost flesh and strength rapidly. With every possible care, horses, accustomed to grain, and to the regular
and plentiful nourishment of the stable and the farm, lose
heart and condition in traveling on the prairies. In all expeditions of the kind we were engaged in, the hardy Indian

horses, which are generally mustangs, or a cross of the wild breed, are to be preferred. They can stand all fatigues, hardships, and privations, and thrive on the grasses and wild herbage of the plains.

Our men, too, had acted with little forethought; galloping off whenever they had a chance, after the game that we encountered while on the march. In this way they had strained and wearied their horses, instead of husbanding their strength and spirits. On a tour of the kind, horses should as seldom as possible be put off of a quiet walk; and the average day's journey should not exceed ten miles.

We had hoped, by pushing forward, to reach the bottoms of the Red River, which abound with young cane, a most nourishing forage for cattle at this season of the year. It would now take us several days to arrive there, and in the meantime many of our horses would probably give out. It was the time, too, when the hunting parties of Indians set fire to the prairies; the herbage, throughout this part of the country, was in that parched state, favorable to combustion, and there was daily more and more risk that the prairies between us and the fort would be set on fire by some of the return parties of Osages, and a scorched desert left for us to traverse. In a word, we had started too late in the season, or loitered too much in the early part of our march, to accomplish our originally intended tour; and there was imminent hazard, if we continued on, that we should lose the greater part of our horses; and, besides suffering various other inconveniences, be obliged to return on foot. It was determined, therefore, to give up all further progress, and, turning our faces to the southeast, to make the best of our way back to Fort Gibson.

This resolution being taken, there was an immediate eagerness to put it into operation. Several horses, however, were missing, and among others those of the captain and the surgeon. Persons had gone in search of them, but the morning advanced without any tidings of them. Our party, in the meantime, being all ready for a march, the commissioner determined to set off in the advance, with his original escort of a lieutenant and fourteen rangers, leaving the captain to come on at his convenience with the main body. At ten o'clock we accordingly started, under the guidance of Beatte, who had hunted over this part of the country and knew the direct route to the garrison.

For some distance we skirted the prairie, keeping a southeast direction; and in the course of our ride we saw a variety of wild animals, deer, white and black wolves, buffaloes, and wild horses. To the latter, our half-breeds and Tonish gave ineffectual chase, only serving to add to the weariness of their already jaded steeds. Indeed it is rarely that any but the weaker and least fleet of the wild horses are taken in these hard racings; while the horse of the huntsman is prone to be knocked up. The latter, in fact, risks a good horse to catch a bad one. On this occasion, Tonish, who was a perfect imp on horseback, and noted for ruining every animal he bestrode, succeeded in laming and almost disabling the powerful gray on which we had mounted him at the outset of our tour.

After proceeding a few miles, we left the prairie, and struck to the east, taking what Beatte pronounced an old Osage war-track. This led us through a rugged tract of country, overgrown with scrubbed forests and entangled thickets, and intersected by deep ravines, and brisk-running streams, the sources of Little River. About three o'clock, we encamped by some pools of water in a small valley, having come about fourteen miles. We had brought on a supply of provisions from our last camp, and supped heartily upon stewed buffalo meat, roasted venison, beignets, or fritters of flour fried in bear's lard, and tea made of a species of the golden-rod, which we had found, throughout our whole route, almost as grateful a beverage as coffee. Indeed our coffee, which, as long as it held out, had been served up with every meal, according to the custom of the West, was by no means a beverage to boast of. It was roasted in a frying-pan, without much care, pounded in a leathern bag, with a round stone, and boiled in our prime and almost only kitchen utensil, the camp kettle, in "branch" or brook water; which, on the prairies, is deeply colored by the soil, of which it always holds abundant particles in a state of solution and suspension. In fact, in the course of our tour, we had tasted the quality of every variety of soil, and the draughts of water we had taken might vie in diversity of color, if not of flavor, with the tinctures of an apothecary's shop. Pure, limpid water is a rare luxury on the prairies, at least at this season of the year. Supper over, we placed sentinels about our scanty and diminished camp, spread our skins and blankets under the trees, now nearly destitute of foliage, and slept soundly until morning.

We had a beautiful daybreak. The camp again resounded with cheerful voices; every one was animated with the thoughts of soon being at the fort, and reveling on bread and vegetables. Even our saturnine man, Beatte, seemed inspired on this occasion; and as he drove up the horses for the march, I heard him singing, in nasal tones, a most forlorn Indian ditty. All this transient gayety, however, soon died away amid the fatigues of our march, which lay through the same kind of rough, hilly, thicketed country as that of yesterday. In the course of the morning we arrived at the valley of the Little River, where it wound through a broad bottom of alluvial soil. At present it had overflowed its banks and inundated a great part of the valley. The difficulty was to distinguish the stream from the broad sheets of water it had formed, and to find a place where it might be forded; for it was in general deep and miry, with abrupt crumbling banks. Under the pilotage of Beatte, therefore, we wandered for some time among the links made by this winding stream, in what appeared to us a trackless labyrinth of swamps, thickets, and standing pools. Sometimes our jaded horses dragged their limbs forward with the utmost difficulty, having to toil for a great distance with the water up to the stirrups, and beset at the bottom with roots and creeping plants. Sometimes we had to force our way through dense thickets of brambles and grapevines, which almost pulled us out of our saddles. In one place, one of the pack-horses sunk in the mire and fell on his side, so as to be extricated with great difficulty. Wherever the soil was bare, or there was a sand-bank, we beheld innumerable tracks of bears, wolves, wild horses, turkeys, and water-fowl; showing the abundant sport this valley might afford to the huntsman. Our men, however, were sated with hunting, and too weary to be excited by these signs, which in the outset of our tour would have put them in a fever of anticipation. Their only desire, at present, was to push on doggedly for the fortress.

At length we succeeded in finding a fording place, where we all crossed Little River, with the water and mire to the saddle-girths, and then halted for an hour and a half, to overhaul the wet baggage, and give the horses time to rest.

On resuming our march, we came to a pleasant little meadow, surrounded by groves of elms and cottonwood trees, in the midst of which was a fine black horse grazing. Beatte, who was in the advance, beckoned us to halt, and, being mounted on a mare, approached the horse gently, step by step, imitating the whinny of the animal with admirable exactness. The noble courser of the prairie gazed for a time, snuffed the air, neighed, pricked up his ears, and pranced round and round the mare in gallant style; but kept at too great a distance for Beatte to throw the lariat. He was a magnificent object, in all the pride and glory of his nature. It was admirable to see the lofty and airy carriage of his head; the freedom of every movement; the elasticity with which he trod the meadow. Finding it impossible to get within noosing distance, and seeing that the horse was receding and growing alarmed, Beatte slid down from his saddle, leveled his rifle across the back of his mare, and took aim, with the evident intention of creasing him. I felt a throb of anxiety for the safety of the noble animal, and called out to Beatte to desist. It was too late; he pulled the trigger as I spoke; luckily he did not shoot with his usual accuracy, and I had the satisfaction to see the coal-black steed dash off unharmed into the forest.

On leaving this valley, we ascended among broken hills and rugged, ragged forests, equally harassing to horse and rider. The ravines, too, were of red clay, and often so steep that, in descending, the horses would put their feet together and fairly slide down, and then scramble up the opposite side like cats. Here and there, among the thickets in the valleys, we met with sloes and persimmon, and the eagerness with which our men broke from the line of march, and ran to gather these poor fruits, showed how much they craved some vegetable condiment, after living so long exclusively on animal food.

About half-past three we encamped near a brook in a meadow, where there was some scanty herbage for our half-famished horses. As Beatte had killed a fat doe in the course of the day, and one of our company a fine turkey, we did not lack for provisions.

It was a splendid autumnal evening. The horizon, after sunset, was of a clear apple green, rising into a delicate lake which gradually lost itself in a deep purple blue. One narrow streak of cloud, of a mahogany color, edged with amber and gold, floated in the west, and just beneath it was the evening star, shining with the pure brilliancy of a diamond. In unison with this scene, there was an evening concert of insects of various kinds, all blended and harmonized into one sober and somewhat melancholy note, which I have always found to have a soothing effect upon the mind, disposing it to quiet musings.

The night that succeeded was calm and beautiful. There was a faint light from the moon, now in its second quarter, and after it had set, a fine starlight, with shooting meteors. The wearied rangers, after a little murmuring conversation round their fires, sank to rest at an early hour, and I seemed to have the whole scene to myself. It is delightful, in thus bivouacking on the prairies, to lie awake and gaze at the stars; it is like watching them from the deck of a ship at sea, when at one view we have the whole cope of heaven. One realizes, in such lonely scenes, that companionship with these beautiful luminaries which made astronomers of the Eastern shepherds, as they watched their flocks by night. How often, while contemplating their mild and benignant radiance, I have called to mind the exquisite text of Job: "Canst thou bind the secret influences of the Pleiades, or loose the bands of Orion?" I do not know why it was, but I felt this night unusually affected by the solemn magnificence of the firmament; and seemed, as I lay thus under the open vault of heaven, to inhale the pure untainted air, and exhilarating buoyancy of spirit, and, as it were, an ecstasy of mind. I slept and waked alternately; and when I slept, my dreams partook of the happy tone of my waking reveries. Toward morning, one of the sentinels, the oldest man in the troop, came and took a seat near me; he was weary and sleepy, and impatient to be relieved. I found he had been gazing at the heavens also, but with different feelings.

"If the stars don't deceive me," said he, "it is near daybreak."

"There can be no doubt of that," said Beatte, who lay close by. "I heard an owl just now."

"Does the owl, then, hoot toward daybreak?" asked I.

"Ay, sir, just as the cock crows."

This was a useful habitude of the bird of wisdom, of which I was not aware. Neither the stars nor owl deceived their votaries. In a short time there was a faint streak of light in the east.

CHAPTER THIRTY-FOUR

OLD CREEK ENCAMPMENT—SCARCITY OF PROVISIONS—BAD
WEATHER—WEARY MARCHING—A HUNTER'S BRIDGE

THE country through which we passed this morning (November 2d) was less rugged and of more agreeable aspect than that we had lately traversed. At eleven o'clock we came out upon an extensive prairie, and about six miles to our left beheld a long line of green forest, marking the course of the north fork of the Arkansas. On the edge of the prairie, and in a spacious grove of noble trees which overshadowed a small brook, were the traces of an old Creek hunting camp. On the bark of the trees were rude delineations of hunters and squaws, scrawled with charcoal; together with various signs and hieroglyphics, which our half-breeds interpreted as indicating that from this encampment the hunters had returned home.

In this beautiful camping ground we made our midday halt. While reposing under the trees, we heard a shouting at no great distance, and presently the captain and the main body of rangers, whom we had left behind two days since, emerged from the thickets, and, crossing the brook, were joyfully welcomed into the camp. The captain and the doctor had been unsuccessful in the search after their horses, and were obliged to march for the greater part of the time on foot; yet they had come on with more than ordinary speed.

We resumed our march about one o'clock, keeping easterly, and approaching the north fork obliquely; it was late before we found a good camping place; the beds of the streams were dry, the prairies, too, had been burned in various places by Indian hunting parties. At length we found water in a small alluvial bottom, where there was tolerable pasturage.

On the following morning there were flashes of lightning in the east, with low, rumbling thunder, and clouds began to gather about the horizon. Beatte prognosticated rain, and that the wind would veer to the north. In the course of our march a flock of brant were seen overhead, flying from the north. "There comes the wind!" said Beatte; and, in fact, it began to blow from that quarter almost immediately, with occasional flurries of rain. About half-past nine o'clock we forded the north fork of the Canadian, and encamped about one, that our hunters might have time to beat up the neighborhood for game; for a serious scarcity began to prevail in the camp. Most of the rangers were young, heedless, and inexperienced, and could not be prevailed upon, while provisions abounded, to provide for the future, by jerking meat, or carrying away any on their horses. On leaving an encampment, they would leave quantities of meat lying about, trusting to Providence and their rifles for a future supply. The consequence was that any temporary scarcity of game, or ill-luck in hunting, produced almost a famine in the camp. In the present instance, they had left loads of buffalo meat at the camp on the great prairie; and having ever since been on a forced march, leaving no time for hunting, they were now destitute of supplies and pinched with hunger. Some had not eaten anything since the morning of the preceding day. Nothing would have persuaded them, when reveling in the abundance of the buffalo encampment, that they would so soon be in such famishing plight.

The hunters returned with indifferent success. The game had been frightened away from this part of the country by Indian hunting parties which had preceded us. Ten or a dozen wild turkeys were brought in, but not a deer had been seen. The rangers began to think turkeys and even prairie hens deserving of attention; game which they had hitherto considered unworthy of their rifles.

The night was cold and windy, with occasional sprinklings of rain; but we had roaring fires to keep us comfortable. In the night, a flight of wild geese passed over the camp, making a great cackling in the air; symptoms of approaching winter.

We set forward at an early hour the next morning, in a northeast course, and came upon the trace of a party of Creek Indians, which enabled our poor horses to travel with more ease. We entered upon a fine champaign country. From a rising ground we had a noble prospect, over extensive prairies, finely diversified by groves and tracts of woodland, and bounded by long lines of distant hills, all clothed with the rich mellow tints of autumn. Game, too, was more plenty. A fine buck sprang up from among the herbage on our right and dashed off at full speed; but a young ranger by the name of Childers, who was on foot, leveled his rifle, discharged a ball that broke the neck of the bounding deer, and sent him tumbling head over heels forward. Another buck and a doe, besides several turkeys, were killed before we came to a halt, so that the hungry mouths of the troop were once more supplied.

About three o'clock we encamped in a grove after a forced march of twenty-five miles, that had proved a hard trial to the horses. For a long time after the head of the line had encamped, the rest kept straggling in, two and three at a time; one of our pack-horses had given out, about nine miles back, and a pony belonging to Beatte shortly after. Many of the other horses looked so gaunt and feeble that doubts were entertained of their being able to reach the fort. In the night there was heavy rain, and the morning dawned cloudy and dismal. The camp resounded, however, with something of its former gayety. The rangers had supped well, and were renovated in spirits, anticipating a speedy arrival at the garrison. Before we set forward on our march, Beatte returned, and brought his pony to the camp with great difficulty. The pack-horse, however, was completely knocked up and had to be abandoned. The wild mare, too, had cast

her foal, through exhaustion, and was not in a state to go
forward. She and the pony, therefore, were left at this encampment, where there was water and good pasturage; and
where there would be a chance of their reviving, and being
afterward sought out and brought to the garrison.

We set off about eight o'clock, and had a day of weary
and harassing travel; part of the time over rough hills, and
part over rolling prairies. The rain had rendered the soil
slippery and plashy, so as to afford unsteady foothold. Some
of the rangers dismounted, their horses having no longer
strength to bear them. We made a halt in the course of the
morning, but the horses were too tired to graze. Several
of them laid down, and there was some difficulty in getting them on their feet again. Our troop presented a
forlorn appearance, straggling slowly along, in a broken
and scattered line that extended over hill and dale, for
three miles and upward, in groups of three and four, widely
apart; some on horseback, some on foot, with a few lag-
gards far in the rear. About four o'clock we halted for the
night in a spacious forest, beside a deep narrow river called
the Little North Fork, or Deep Creek. It was late before
the main part of the troop straggled into the encampment,
many of the horses having given out. As this stream was
too deep to be forded we waited until the next day to devise
means to cross it; but our half-breeds swam the horses of
our party to the other side in the evening, as they would
have better pasturage, and the stream was evidently swelling. The night was cold and unruly; the wind sounding
hoarsely through the forest and whirling about the dry
leaves. We made long fires of great trunks of trees, which
diffused something of consolation if not cheerfulness around.

The next morning there was general permission given to
hunt until twelve o'clock; the camp being destitute of provisions. The rich woody bottom in which we were encamped
abounded with wild turkeys, of which a considerable number
were killed. In the meantime, preparations were made for
crossing the river, which had risen several feet during the

night; and it was determined to fell trees for the purpose, to serve as bridges.

The captain and doctor, and one or two other leaders of the camp, versed in woodcraft, examined, with learned eye, the trees growing on the river bank, until they singled out a couple of the largest size and most suitable inclinations. The ax was then vigorously applied to their roots, in such a way as to insure their falling directly across the stream. As they did not reach to the opposite bank, it was necessary for some of the men to swim across and fell trees on the other side, to meet them. They at length succeeded in making a precarious footway across the deep and rapid current, by which the baggage could be carried over; but it was necessary to grope our way, step by step, along the trunks and main branches of the trees, which for a part of the distance were completely submerged, so that we were to our waists in water. Most of the horses were then swum across, but some of them were too weak to brave the current, and evidently too much knocked up to bear any further travel. Twelve men, therefore, were left at the encampment to guard these horses, until, by repose and good pasturage, they should be sufficiently recovered to complete their journey; and the captain engaged to send the men a supply of flour and other necessaries as soon as we should arrive at the fort.

***

CHAPTER THIRTY-FIVE

A LOOKOUT FOR LAND—HARD TRAVELING AND HUNGRY HALTING—A FRONTIER FARMHOUSE—ARRIVAL AT THE GARRISON

IT was a little after one o'clock when we again resumed our weary wayfaring. The residue of that day and the whole of the next were spent in toilsome travel. Part of the way was over stony hills, part across wide prairies, rendered spongy and miry by the recent rain, and cut up by brooks swollen into torrents. Our poor horses were so feeble that it was with difficulty we could get them across the deep ravines and turbulent streams. In traversing the miry plains, they slipped and staggered at every step, and most of us were obliged to dismount and walk for the greater part of the way. Hunger prevailed throughout the troop; every one began to look anxious and haggard, and to feel the growing length of each additional mile. At one time, in crossing a hill, Beatte climbed a high tree, commanding a wide prospect, and took a lookout, like a mariner from the masthead at sea. He came down with cheering tidings. To the left he had beheld a line of forest stretching across the country, which he knew to be the woody border of the Arkansas; and at a distance he had recognized certain landmarks, from which he concluded that we could not be above forty miles distant from the fort. It was like the welcome cry of land to tempest-tossed mariners.

In fact we soon after saw smoke rising from a woody glen at a distance. It was supposed to be made by a hunting-party of Creek or Osage Indians from the neighborhood of the fort, and was joyfully hailed as a harbinger of man. It was now confidently hoped that we would soon arrive among the frontier hamlets of Creek Indians, which are scattered along the skirts of the uninhabited wilderness; and our hungry rangers trudged forward with reviving spirit, regaling themselves with savory anticipations of farmhouse luxuries, and enumerating every article of good cheer, until their mouths fairly watered at the shadowy feasts thus conjured up.

A hungry night, however, colsed in upon a toilsome day. We encamped on the border of one of the tributary streams of the Arkansas, amid the ruins of a stately grove that had been riven by a hurricane. The blast had torn its way through the forest in a narrow column, and its course was marked by enormous trees shivered and splintered, and upturned, with their roots in the air; all lay in one direction, like so many brittle reeds broken and trodden down by the hunter.

Here was fuel in abundance, without the labor of the ax; we had soon immense fires blazing and sparkling in the frosty air, and lighting up the whole forest; but, alas! we had no meat to cook at them. The scarcity in the camp almost amounted to famine. Happy was he who had a morsel of jerked meat, or even the half-picked bones of a former repast. For our part, we were more lucky at our mess than our neighbors; one of our men having shot a turkey. We had no bread to eat with it, nor salt to season it withal. It was simply boiled in water; the latter was served up as soup, and we were fain to rub each morsel of the turkey on the empty salt-bag, in hopes some saline particle might remain to relieve its insipidity.

The night was biting cold; the brilliant moonlight sparkled on the frosty crystals which covered every object around us. The water froze beside the skins on which we bivouacked, and in the morning I found the blanket in which I was wrapped covered with a hoar frost; yet I had never slept more comfortably.

After a shadow of a breakfast, consisting of turkey bones and a cup of coffee without sugar, we decamped at an early hour; for hunger is a sharp quickener on a journey. The prairies were all gemmed with frost, that covered the tall weeds and glistened in the sun. We saw great flights of prairie-hens or grouse, that hovered from tree to tree, or sat in rows along the naked branches, waiting until the sun should melt the frost from the weeds and herbage. Our rangers no longer despised such humble game, but turned from the ranks in pursuit of a prairie-hen as eagerly as they formerly would go in pursuit of a deer.

Every one now pushed forward, anxious to arrive at some human habitation before night. The poor horses were urged beyond their strength, in the thought of soon being able to indemnify them for present toil, by rest and ample provender. Still the distances seemed to stretch out more than ever, and

the blue hills, pointed out as landmarks on the horizon, to
recede as we advanced. Every step became a labor; every
now and then a miserable horse would give out and lie down.
His owner would raise him by main strength, force him forward to the margin of some stream, where there might be a
scanty border of herbage, and then abandon him to his fate.
Among those that were thus left on the way was one of the
led horses of the count; a prime hunter, that had taken the
lead of everything in the chase of the wild horses. It was
intended, however, as soon as we should arrive at the fort,
to send out a party provided with corn, to bring in such of
the horses as should survive.

In the course of the morning we came upon Indian tracks,
crossing each other in various directions, a proof that we
must be in the neighborhood of human habitations. At
length, on passing through a skirt of wood, we beheld two
or three log houses, sheltered under lofty trees on the border
of a prairie, the habitations of Creek Indians, who had small
farms adjacent. Had they been sumptuous villas, abounding with the luxuries of civilization, they could not have
been hailed with greater delight.

Some of the rangers rode up to them in quest of food; the
greater part, however, pushed forward in search of the habitation of a white settler, which we were told was at no great
distance. The troop soon disappeared among the trees, and
I followed slowly in their track; for my once fleet and generous steed faltered under me, and was just able to drag one
foot after the other, yet I was too weary and exhausted to
spare him.

In this way we crept on, until, on turning a thick clump
of trees, a frontier farmhouse suddenly presented itself to
view. It was a low tenement of logs, overshadowed by great
forest trees, but it seemed as if a very region of Cocaigne prevailed around it. Here was a stable and barn, and granaries
teeming with abundance, while legions of grunting swine,
gobbling turkeys, cackling hens and strutting roosters,
swarmed about the farmyard.

My poor jaded and half-famished horse raised his head and pricked up his ears at the well-known sights and sounds, He gave a chuckling inward sound, something like a dry laugh; whisked his tail, and made great leeway toward a corn-crib, filled with golden ears of maize, and it was with some difficulty that I could control his course, and steer him up to the door of the cabin. A single glance within was sufficient to raise every gastronomic faculty. There sat the captain of the rangers and his officers, round a three-legged table, crowned by a broad and smoking dish of boiled beef and turnips. I sprang off my horse in an instant, cast him loose to make his way to the corn-crib, and entered this palace of plenty. A fat good-humored negress received me at the door. She was the mistress of the house, the spouse of the white man, who was absent. I hailed her as some swart fairy of the wild, that had suddenly conjured up a banquet in the desert; and a banquet was it in good sooth. In a twinkling she lugged from the fire a huge iron pot, that might have rivaled one of the famous flesh-pots of Egypt, or the witches' caldron in "Macbeth." Placing a brown earthen dish on the floor, she inclined the corpulent caldron on one side, and out leaped sundry great morsels of beef, with a regiment of turnips tumbling after them, and a rich cascade of broth overflowing the whole. This she handed me with an ivory smile that extended from ear to ear; apologizing for our humble fare, and the humble style in which it was served up. Humble fare! humble style! Boiled beef and turnips, and an earthen dish to eat them from! To think of apologizing for such a treat to a half-starved man from the prairies; and then such magnificent slices of bread and butter! Head of Apicius, what a banquet!

"The rage of hunger" being appeased, I began to think of my horse. He, however, like an old campaigner, had taken good care of himself. I found him paying assiduous attention to the crib of Indian corn, and dexterously drawing forth and munching the ears that protruded between the bars. It was with great regret that I interrupted his repast, which he abandoned with a heavy sigh, or rather a rumbling groan. I was anxious, however, to rejoin my traveling companions, who had passed by the farmhouse without stopping, and proceeded to the banks of the Arkansas; being in hopes of arriving before night at the Osage Agency. Leaving the captain and his troop, therefore, amid the abundance of the farm, where they had determined to quarter themselves for the night, I bade adieu to our sable hostess, and again pushed forward.

A ride of about a mile brought me to where my comrades were waiting on the banks of the Arkansas, which here poured along between beautiful forests. A number of Creek Indians, in their brightly colored dresses, looking like so many gay tropical birds, were busy aiding our men to transport the baggage across the river in a canoe. While this was doing, our horses had another regale from two great cribs heaped up with ears of Indian corn, which stood near the edge of the river. We had to keep a check upon the poor half-famished animals, lest they should injure themselves by their voracity.

The baggage being all carried to the opposite bank, we embarked in the canoe, and swum our horses across the river I was fearful lest in their enfeebled state they should not be able to stem the current; but their banquet of Indian corn had already infused fresh life and spirit into them, and it would appear as if they were cheered by the instinctive consciousness of their approach to home, where they would soon be at rest, and in plentiful quarters; for no sooner had we landed and resumed our route than they set off on a hand-gallop, and continued so for a great part of seven miles that we had to ride through the woods.

It was an early hour in the evening when we arrived at the Agency, on the banks of the Verdigris River, whence we had set off about a month before. Here we passed the night comfortably quartered; yet, after having been accustomed to sleep in the open air, the confinement of a chamber was, in some respects, irksome. The atmosphere seemed close, and destitute of freshness; and when I woke in the night and gazed about me upon complete darkness, I missed the glorious companionship of the stars.

The next morning, after breakfast, I again set forward, in company with the worthy commissioner, for Fort Gibson, where we arrived much tattered, travel-stained, and weather-beaten, but in high health and spirits; and thus ended my foray into the Pawnee Hunting Grounds.